The
8 Practices
of Exceptional
Companies

The
8 Practices
of Exceptional
Companies

How
Great Organizations
Make the Most of Their
Human Assets

Jac Fitz-enz

American Management Association

New York • Atlanta • Boston • Chicago • Kansas City • San Francisco • Washington, D.C.
Brussels • Mexico City • Tokyo • Toronto

Library of Congress Cataloging-in-Publication Data

Fitz-enz, Jac.
    The 8 practices of exceptional companies : how great organizations make the most of their human assets / Jac Fitz-enz.
        p.   cm.
    Includes bibliographical references and index.
    ISBN 0-8144-0348-4
    1. Organizational effectiveness—Case studies.   2. Benchmarking (Management)—Case studies.   I. Title.
    HD58.9.F578   1997
    658—dc21   96—40876
                                                          CIP

Printing number

10   9   8   7   6   5   4   3   2   1

To
Michael Christopher Fitz-enz
1962–1995.
Mike, you deserved better.
We'll never forget you.

Contents

The
8 Practices
of Exceptional
Companies

Introduction

Best Practices
That Add Value

He who will not apply new remedies must expect new evils—
for time is the greatest innovator.

—*Francis Bacon*
"*Of Innovations,*" The Essays

The search for effective management practices is not new. Business executives have always wanted to know not only how well the competition is doing but what it is doing and how it is doing it. Best practice research is not new. The Japanese used the process very effectively after World War II to refute U.S. Secretary of State John Foster Dulles's 1955 assertion that the United States would always enjoy a trade surplus with Japan because Japanese products were so inferior.[1]

In 1989, Robert Camp, a quality manager at Xerox, wrote the book that gave the process the name of benchmarking and kicked off a frenzy of activity.[2] Suddenly, everyone wanted to benchmark best practices even when they didn't fully understand the methodology. Today, for many people the terms *best practices* and *benchmarking* mean simply comparative performance research.

My Objectives

Although best practices and benchmarking have become intertwined topics for some people, this book is not a discussion of benchmarking. Instead, it is a discussion of our findings and opinions based on research into how effective companies manage the "human asset"—the people whose efforts are the basis of any organization's success. To manage an asset you first have to acquire it, then maintain it, then—in the case of the human asset—develop it and direct it. Human asset acquisition involves work force planning, succession planning, hiring, and orienting. Maintenance covers pay, benefits, employee and labor relations, information and communications systems, and retention. Development deals with training, learning experiences of all types, and career management. Direction has to do with scheduling, problem solving and disciplining, and perhaps termination. Collectively, these activities take up a large percentage of a manager's time and, depending on the type of business, consume anywhere from 20 percent to 70 percent of revenues. That is what I'm going to talk to you about.

This book is designed to serve two purposes. The first is to present the best human asset management practices that my organization, the Saratoga Institute, uncovered during a four-year study of over 1,000 companies. We learned that what constitutes best practice is an interactive set of eight organizational characteristics. These are the antecedent traits and beliefs that drive the *formulation* of the admirable human management processes that are easily and often observed—for example, a particular compensation or employee development program. These characteristics, not their visible programmatic manifestations, constitute the best human asset management practices. The Saratoga Institute research program buried the idea that a best management practice is a specific process, project, or program.

My second objective is to expose the wasteful and misleading practices that cause three out of four improvement projects to fall short of their goals. I am offering a proven business research method founded on objective data in place of the aimless wandering that sometimes passes for best practice benchmarking. This is an important problem for businesspeople because millions of dollars are wasted annually on improvement projects that yield little value. In a report on the popularity of benchmarking junkets, *Business Week* pointed out that many "best practice workshops and visits are so brief, superficial, and stage-managed that they amount to little more than industrial tourism."[3]

Validation

Coincident with the preparation of this manuscript, I read *Built to Last* by James Collins and Jerry Porras. The authors describe their study of organizational and management practices in thirty-six companies. Their research team compared the best-performing companies in eighteen industries against eighteen others that were nearly as good—the number-one and number-two companies, respectively, in the industry. They were "looking for underlying, timeless, fundamental principles and patterns" that might differentiate the pairs. The number-one company was called the visionary organization. Distinct differences between the two were found along several dimensions. They summarized the differences as "the success of visionary companies—at least in part—as coming from underlying processes and fundamental dynamics embedded in the organization. . . ."[4]

Several of their factors correlated with our findings. In addition, we uncovered three others that they did not see. We found that communications, partnering, and collective support systems contributed to maintaining long-term exceptional performance and how they did so.

Not All and Not Perfect

The research underlying this book does not stem from every major company in the United States or from their counterparts in the other countries mentioned. We started in 1991 with 573 companies and have now covered over 1,000 in the United States, Australia, Brazil, Canada, Malaysia, Mexico, Singapore, the United Kingdom, and Venezuela. We have been approached by the People's Republic of China to open a performance management institute in Beijing and there apply our methods to China's growing industrial base. This will give us an entirely different culture and political system within which to continue our research.

Inclusion in our research population is voluntary. Therefore, some of the famous companies that have garnered a great deal of publicity are not cited, whereas many firms you may never have heard of are included. Our companies range in size from about 300 employees to more than 50,000. We've noticed over the years that much of the most effective and innovative work is being done in the unheralded midsize organizations. These are the ones that are eager to overtake the market giants.

The companies I cite are not without problems. Like others, they are inhabited by human beings who from time to time make poor decisions. What distinguishes these companies is that they qualify by having met a rigorous set of quantitative human and financial performance criteria. There are no nominations. Objective performance is the only way in. The companies that qualify as best practice exemplars represent the top 5 percent of our population.

At the End of the Day

Anyone can publish unsubstantiated stories of so-called best practices. There are plenty on the market. This book does not imply that our research into best practices has ended. It will go on as far into the future as we can foresee. We would like to hear readers' reactions to our findings, so I ask you to view the material that follows in the light of your own experience. Does it ring true at the common-sense level? Is it substantive? Does it support some of your suspicions about the hoopla that accompanies popular management prescriptions of the here-today, gone-tomorrow variety? My almost forty years in business along with my work in this ongoing effort tell me that there is fundamental truth to our findings. My direct contact with the people described has been a rich learning experience. I hope that this attempt to describe it will be useful to you.

Acknowledgments

This book is a tribute to the collective efforts of many people. First are the thousands in the best-practice companies who did the sterling work described here. Second are my associates at the Saratoga Institute and our international representatives. Both groups have labored to introduce value-adding methods and to build the longitudinal databases on which our study is based. I am especially indebted to Peter Howes in Australia, Abdul Rahim Majid in Malaysia, Alfonso Gonzales in Mexico, and Maurice and Richard Phelps—father and son—in the United Kingdom. These visionaries were the first outside the United States to embrace this objective approach to best management practices. Next are friends and professional associates who over the years have encouraged me and supported the work of the Saratoga Institute—people like Dave Ulrich at the University of Michigan, a good friend and brilliant analyst, and Ron Pilenzo and Mike Losey, CEOs of the Society for Human Resource Management, which has sponsored our research since it began in 1985. I also thank various staff members at the American Management Association, especially Adrienne Hickey, who provided excellent, incisive editorial guidance. Neither last nor least is my partner and wife, Ellen Kieffer, a source of constant joy and inspiration who gave me valuable insight on our findings just when it was most needed. Finally, I dedicate this book to my son, Mike, who passed away during its preparation. He was one of the bravest men I've ever known and I'll never let his memory die.

References

1. Alfred E. Eckes, "Trading American Interests," *Foreign Affairs*, Fall 1992, pp. 135–154.
2. Robert Camp, *Benchmarking: The Search for Industry Best Practices That Lead to Superior Performance* (Milwaukee: ASQC Press, 1989).
3. "Management Meccas," *Business Week* (September 18, 1995), p. 126.
4. James C. Collins and Jerry I. Porras, *Built to Last* (New York: HarperCollins, 1994), p. 41.

1

From Paradox
to Best Practices

*The Real Difference
Between the Best and the Rest*

paradox: inconsistency, incongruity, contradiction
—American Collegiate Dictionary

In *The Age of Paradox*, Charles Handy stated that paradox is an endemic, inevitable part of life.[1] He's right. Most of us accept and deal with paradox every day, often without thinking about it. Paradox has been explained in the laws of physics: For every action there is an equal and opposite reaction. We also experience it in our personal relationships when we hurt the ones we love the most. Paradox is everywhere, but nowhere is it more evident than in large organizations. When we consider the basic issues confronting management today, we see how, simultaneously, managers have to think global and act local, be individualistic while joining the team, delegate and still control, centralize and decentralize, administer and outsource. It's no wonder that we are confused when it comes to seeking best practices in human asset management.

In the information or knowledge era, the most powerful and distinguishing asset of every institution is its people. This is not a platitude. Cash, facilities, equipment, and material—including databases—are all inert. High returns on their investment are totally dependent on human actions. When the efficiency of the input-transformation-output process relies primarily on the flow of information, the human asset is the driving force. From this time forward, success is spelled k-n-o-w-l-e-d-g-e. Knowledge converts data into information. And we use information to activate all other assets, including ourselves. Management's imperative is to help its human assets become knowledgeable. This starts with a clear understanding of the enterprise's values and strategy. It includes forming a coherent, innovative culture, communicating everything necessary, training people in how to work together effectively, and never settling for less than their best efforts. No amount of capital will be enough to offset the absence of knowledgeable, motivated people. Organizations that can find the tools and build the systems for effective human asset management will be the winners.

The Nature of Paradox

The search for best human asset management practices is hindered by two process paradoxes boxed inside a contextual paradox, as illustrated in Figure 1-1. It's something akin to, although not as serious as, Churchill's claim that "Russia is a riddle, wrapped in a mystery, inside an enigma."[2]

If industrial engineer Frederick Taylor's search for the one best way to do a given task was discredited eighty years ago, why are we still looking for "the" answer? It is because, as Einstein supposedly said, "There is nothing so practical as a good theory." Please note that a theory is not a speculation; a speculation is a hypothesis. A theory can be held to explain a phenomenon when there is a body of demonstrable evidence supporting it. In the case of benchmarking, the hope of managers has been that in studying the work of others who are allegedly the best at a process, some transferable truths will emerge. When that elusive goal is realized, nothing is more valuable.

The *theory* this book illustrates involves eight elemental factors that have proved themselves to be organizational management truths. Over a four-year period these eight have repeatedly turned up as the common management practices among the top 5 percent of our 1,000 companies studied. In the course of this work the para-

Figure 1-1. Best-practice paradox boxes.

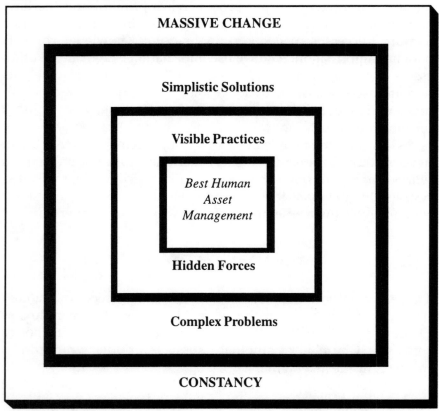

doxes emerged. In order to fully understand the importance of the organizational drivers that follow it is necessary briefly to outline the paradoxes of best-practice benchmarking.

Process Paradoxes

One process paradox has to do with the investigative method. "All that glitters is not gold" is an axiom of ancient and unknown origin. This distinction explains the magic wand approach, otherwise known as simplistic solutions to complicated problems. It is an illustration of some managers' attempts to improve their organizations. Sincere and well-meaning people by the thousands are jumping on board the latest vehicle in the hope of gaining ground in the never-ending race for competitive advantage. According to estimates drawn from several major U.S. consulting firms, the probability of success is about one in four.

So long as we persist in this naive approach, the quest for best practices will be an inherently fruitless pursuit. We're never going to locate the best practice—the magic bullet—until we acknowledge that neat solutions for complex puzzles won't be found in quick calls or visits to other companies. Conversely, best-practice research can be an eminently practical activity. Done well, it usually enables us to learn something. The difference between great learning and misunderstanding frequently lies in the investigative process. Like most other things in life, how you do it is as important as what you do.

The other process paradox stems from a surprising discovery about the nature of a best practice: Those cases that are generally reported as best practices aren't best practices! If you take the time and trouble to check them out, you will find that many of the projects and programs that have been published as best practices are arbitrary, overstated, transient, and nearly always only the visible manifestations of something much more fundamental. True best human asset management is a mix of primary forces that shape the visible processes.

The task of uncovering the best involves separating the enduring truths from mere fanciful tales. Most recountings of effective management practices are the result of reporting rather than research. The management of human beings is an intricate art form, as anyone who has tried it will attest. So, it is obvious that best management practices do not reveal themselves to surface reporting. The reporter approach most often yields half-truths, which in turn lead to misunderstanding and misapplication. The search for generalizable management principles demands research. Packaging fanciful tales with eye-catching graphics does not make them sound. Popularity is also not a test of validity. To paraphrase British mathematician and philosopher Alfred North Whitehead, carrying an invalid statistic to three decimal places doesn't make it any more valid.

The Mother of All Paradoxes

Just as generals are often accused of fighting the last war rather than the present one, we managers are chided for dealing with the past or present rather than the future. We must face up to the elemental changes currently affecting our workplaces. Trying to respond to today's and tomorrow's problems with yesterday's solutions is the most injurious of paradoxes. It ensures that we will misconstrue and misplay our opportunities.

Economist Jeremy Rifkin claims that in the United States 90 million out of 124 million jobs are vulnerable to being replaced by machines.[3] Since the 1950s, blue-collar jobs in the United States have been dropping from 33 percent of the total to the less than 12 percent that is estimated for them early in the next decade.[4] White-collar jobs aren't safe either. In the past decade alone, over 3 million staff jobs have been eliminated. Yet Rifkin estimates that only about 5 percent of the companies worldwide have even begun to make the transition to the Information Age. That Age will ride on electronic technology rather than human physical strength. In fact, it already does. Redesigning Information Age systems on the basis of Industrial Age technology is absurdly naive.

We all recognize that humans are being replaced by smart machines. To accommodate this, William Bridges, in his study *Job Shift*, points out that holding on to the job as an element of production is out of date. His premise is that jobs ought to be replaced with a more holistic construct of work processes driven by the market rather than by the organization. This notion has yet to be accepted in most companies. The conclusion must be that benchmarking yesterday's job-based practices doesn't put us ahead of the curve for tomorrow's market-process world. Bridges argues for redesigning the whole production system around the customer's needs rather than around jobs and processes.[5] This strikes at the heart of the search for best practices. By emulating even the best of the past we build greater barriers to future effectiveness.

The incongruity is glaring when you look at best-practice reports that focus on rearranging an old idea for a new situation. It's like moving the same set or number of chairs (jobs) into different alignment. The problem is not how we can cut down on the number of chairs or what a more efficient formation might be. In the future, there won't be time to sit in chairs. All personnel doing skilled work will be constantly on the move, probably with a portable, voice-activated electronic instrument that functions as their workplace. It will be, "Have skills, will travel."

If Rifkin and Bridges are even remotely correct in their predictions, the resolution of this central paradox will be found in recognizing that the massive change in the world is more than a business issue. Changes in technology are mixing with political, social, and economic forces to restructure organizations and create the world of the twenty-first century. As I pointed out in my book *Human Value Management*, it's evolutionary change coming at revolutionary speed.[6] The transformation from the industrial to the informational world is moving at the speed of light compared to the transformation from the agricultural to the industrial world. In such a massively disrupted environment the best-practice response must be so fundamental, so near the bedrock of human interaction, that it will play as effectively in 2050 as it does in 1997.

The Secret of Best Practice

If best practice is not to be found in the way a policy, system, or process is structured or carried out within another organization, where is it hiding? That common, externally focused approach is driven by a mind-set that looks outside the organization for a solution. The secret of best practice is to focus internally. The truth lies within. We start by asking ourselves if there are basic guidelines to organizational effectiveness that apply in any situation. Such an elemental notion is easier to grasp if we take it outside the company with an analogy to human health. All human creation is nothing more than a manifestation of itself—its values, beliefs, skills, and desires. Therefore, analyzing the principles of human health and energy should give us some idea of the principles of organizational health and effectiveness.

The human body faces dangers every day just as does a company. We can take either of two approaches to being healthy. One is to do nothing until we are in some level of chronic discomfort. However, this reactive routine doesn't solve the underlying problem that caused the discomfort. It brings only temporary relief. Until we understand and address the cause, the pain will return in one form or another. Many people live this way. It is inefficient and uncomfortable, to say the least.

With this method we either wait until we are sick or ask someone else what they do to feel well. Neither choice promotes consistent health. The first is totally reactive. The second isn't much better because what one person does to stay healthy is probably going to be only marginally effective for anyone else. No two people are exactly the same and therefore one person's level of exercise or caloric consumption is not necessarily ideal for another. Either way, one could not support these as good health practices.

The other approach to health management is more positive, efficient, and proactive. In this case, we aim to establish, maintain, or improve our state of health. We seek information on how the organism, the body, operates and what it needs to function at a high level of efficiency. Basic guidelines for leading a healthy life have been discovered and published. However, even these cannot always be applied without personal modification. They may have to be altered to suit our physiology and genetic makeup. Once our particular circumstances are acknowledged, we can plan our health practices. These must be followed in a consistent and regular manner. Along the way we monitor the state of our health to confirm that we are not in pain and are energetic and happy.

Organizations also have two options to effective management practices. One is the typical approach, which is to wait until something happens in the marketplace and then react to it. This path includes benchmarking best practices in the hope of finding a process that can be adapted to our situation. If we're lucky, we may locate a remedy that lowers the organization's fever in one function or helps it overcome a current cramp in the system. The problem with this approach is that it is a one-purpose pill. The next time we face a slightly different challenge in the same area we have to go out and benchmark (find a new pill) all over again. We took an analgesic tablet, but we didn't learn the truth about organizational health.

A better method is to find the basic truths of organizational health and effectiveness and commit ourselves to a consistent and persistent regimen. This is what we've witnessed the most effective companies doing. It seems fair to claim that when one applies a consistent, validated method to studying nearly a thousand companies over several years, and repeatedly observes the same driving forces among the top performers, there must be a kernel of truth in the findings.

What these studies provided was overwhelming evidence that the visible programs and processes carried out by the companies were *not* the best practices. They were merely the result of invisible antecedents that determined how those surface activities were structured. In actuality, an exceptionally effective management practice is not an isolated activity. The very term *best practice* is misleading. It suggests some sort of magic wand. It is the grand-child of Frederick Taylor's one-best-way quest. The paradoxes of the current marketplace hide many facts. The most essential truth is that best practice is a cohesive, holistic approach to organiza-tional management. It is a modus operandi built on a central vi-sion. It precedes the visible activity that many have mistaken for best practice. Now, we can see its true nature.

> *The best human asset management practice is an enduring commitment to a set of drivers: basic beliefs, traits, and operat-ing stratagems. These are the constant context of the organiza-tion, the causal forces. They are what identify the best human asset management organizations.*

For short, the companies that have qualified as the best human asset managers in our population are called BHAMs.

Best Human Asset Management as Context

Organizations are multifaceted places in which there are many forces cooperating and conflicting at any one moment. This is the basic reason why it is virtually impossible to *prove* anything in a work environment. But that fact has been extrapolated to create the belief that we can't even measure the return on investment in many human-based activities, and this most definitely is not true. But because we believe our own myths we seldom set up experi-ments in which the majority of variables can be accounted for, much less controlled. Yet there is ample evidence that a well-constructed study in a business environment can reveal previously hidden driving forces.

In our case, we were able to identify factors that were consistent over time, common to a large population, and correlatable with financial performance. I don't claim that these are the sole and eternal truths on which mankind's salvation rests. But I do have evidence that companies featuring the following characteristics consistently outperform others over the long term in both human and financial indices. There are eight driving forces that make up the context from which the best human asset management systems and processes are derived:[7]

❑ **Value.** There is a constant focus on adding value to everything rather than on simply doing something. In addition, there is a conscious, ongoing attempt to balance human and financial values. This is not just a good intention; it is the common practice.

❑ **Commitment.** Management is dedicated to a long-term core strategy. It seeks to build an enduring institution. It is more than open to change; in fact, it seeks it. Conversely, in these BHAMs there is a noticeable avoidance of the temptation to chase after every management fad that comes along.

❑ **Culture.** One of the more distinguishing features of the BHAMs is their proactive application of the corporate culture. Management is aware of how culture and systems can be linked together for consistency and efficiency. That interface is consciously and actively managed.

❑ **Communication.** There is an extraordinary concern for communicating with all stakeholders. Within these organizations, constant and extensive two-way communication is the rule. They use all available media and share all types of vital information with employees and other stakeholders.

❑ **Partnering With Stakeholders.** New market conditions and customer requirements demand new forms of operation. Partnering is the most prominent new form. The BHAMs involve partners both within and outside the company in many decisions. This includes the design and implementation of new programs.

❑ **Collaboration.** There is a high level of collaboration among, and involvement of, all sections *within* functions. The BHAMs study, redesign, launch, and follow up new programs in a collective manner. This includes collective support across sections enhancing cohesiveness and providing a solid front against attacks from outside.

❑ **Innovation and Risk.** Radical change is not frightening here. There is a willingness to shake up the organization to the extent of shutting down the old structure and rebuilding it in a totally different form. Risk and innovation are recognized as necessities in a volatile marketplace.

❑ **Competitive Passion.** The BHAMs are never satisfied. They constantly search for improvements. They set up systems and processes to actively seek out and incorporate ideas from all sources. In every case their motto is, "Wait till you see what we do next."

The Common Thread

Every company that qualified as a best management organization showed these contextual forces. Some were stronger in one force than in others. Each firm put them together in its own way. But most important, all of the factors were prominent in every company.

The obvious question is, "Don't you find traits like these in all or most good companies?" Many of the 1,000 companies that we studied but that did not qualify for best-practice recognition are fine organizations. However, the best practice factors were not as evident in their case, and in some cases were reversed.

For example, the driving focus on adding value and the appreciation for people as well as money was not evident in many of these firms. More often, it was either not visible or given lip service only. Long-term strategic commitment was seldom found. Instead, short-term financial goals took the place of a drive to build an institution of value. There was seldom a visible, conscious attempt to connect culture with systems. Culture was either ignored or not actively incorporated into plans. As a rule, information was not widely shared with the rank and file. The traditional view was that most people didn't need to know. New programs and changes were often dictated rather than built through partnerships. That overused word *empowerment* often had a very small field of play. The concept was not understood nor effectively applied. Collaboration and collective support were clearly not the standard. Internecine rivalries and battles were the rule of the day. Risk was not acknowledged as a preferred modus operandi. While management often talked about people stepping up to making decisions and being creative, experience had taught them not to volunteer. There was a sense of satisfaction after a small success and no apparent sense of the urgent need for constant improvement. The belief was that once a change was successfully put into place it was okay to rest for a while.

In many organizations there were strong visible barriers to BHAM practices. Structural, cultural, and personal characteristics worked against organizational improvement. Few companies exhibited a high level of sustained commitment, efficiency, and team spirit across the organization. The nice words at the front of the annual report did not come to life in daily operations. By contrast, the BHAMs exuded a positive, cooperative attitude backed up by considerable functional management skill. When we looked at the financial performance of the BHAMs, we found that they typically stood in the top percentiles of their industry.

Interaction

One of the clearest points is that the eight factors do not operate independently of each other. They are very interactive, some to the point where it is difficult to distinguish where one stops and the other starts. In actuality, they don't have boundaries. This may account for their having functioned for so long without being noticed. Values permeate an organization just as an aroma is distributed through the atmosphere. Both blend with their surroundings and leave sometimes subtle but powerful evidence. Culture is obviously a corporatewide phenomenon even though each business unit may have its own subculture and methods of communication that reach out across the organization. Graphically, it looks something like Figure 1-2.

Figure 1-2. Interaction of best human asset management factors.

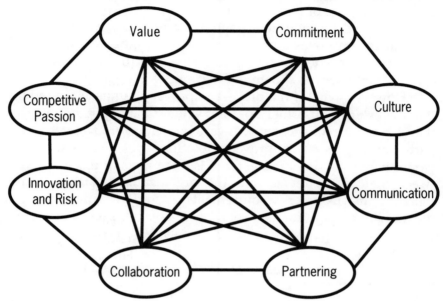

Barriers to Best Practices

Many organizations hamper their search for best practices by their own actions. Three factors serve to block good best-practice benchmarking.

1. *Obsession with action.* Managers in most Western nations are rewarded for activity rather than analysis. In the past forty years the person who seemed to advance most rapidly through the organization was the one who fired a fusillade of arrows into the organizational air, took credit for the few that apparently hit a target, and disavowed responsibility for the others that didn't. Few executives seemed interested in weighing how much invisible damage was done against the visible value gained. Despite the publicity to the contrary, many employees tell us that this practice is still prevalent.

2. *Process fixation.* We have been taught by the quality gurus that if we improve processes we will naturally improve our com-

petitive advantage. This is the half-truth that is partially responsible for the failure of many quality programs. We are looking at the market from the wrong standpoint. It is true that if an internal staff department improves a process, the change should flow through its internal customer processes and eventually out the door to the external customer, as shown in Figure 1-3.

However, what if the process improvement affects something that the external customer does not value? One might assume that the customer's requirement is always known before an internal department begins an improvement effort. But this assumption would be wrong. In practice, there is often a major disconnect between staff departments and the organization's business and, therefore, its customers' requirements. A staff vice president told me that her corporation had set as its five-year target to be among the top five companies in earnings per share in its industry. When

Figure 1-3. Process to customer satisfaction connection.

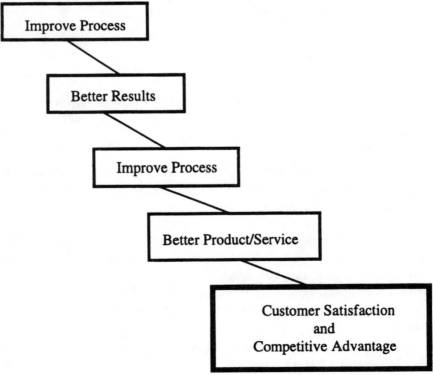

I asked her what corporate earnings were now and what the company's current rank was, she didn't know. Further probing showed that she really wasn't connected to the company's operations even though she sat in on many executive-level meetings.

3. *Lack of skill.* Although every student in business school takes courses in accounting and some form of financial analysis, there is a marked paucity of training in process assessment and evaluation. Over the past eighteen years I have taught performance analysis, measurement, and evaluation to more than 40,000 managers and professionals in two dozen countries. In this program we look at cost, time, quantity, quality, and human reaction data. The objective is to connect internal activity with organizational service, quality, and productivity improvements. Many times the simplest connections are not apparent to even the more seasoned management students. Despite a good deal of explanation, many don't recognize inferential and correlational evidence. They can't build a logical series of questions that lead directly from the subjective concept to the visible, objective result. When it comes to operational factors, insight regarding patterns is absent. Given this lack of capability, along with misdirection and the overwhelming "bias for action," it is predictable that most of our attempts at improvement yield little more than confusion and additional stress.

The Solution

Process improvement and competitive advantage are not all that difficult if you commit yourself to paying the price. There is an investment that cannot be avoided. Our experience tells us that the following imperatives must be served:

1. *Start with training.* Begin by training the people who will be conducting benchmarking or other forms of performance assessment and evaluation. Select a methodology that you like and train everyone on that model. Failing to do this will put you in the same boat the Ford Motor Company found itself in in the mid-1990s. An audit of its quality program showed that more than fifty different quality improvement systems were operating simultaneously throughout the company. As people moved from one unit to

another, they had to be retrained each time, costing the company millions in lost time and direct expense.

2. *Do it right the first time.* If you are not in a position to spend the time and money on conducting a proper study, then don't even start one. The predictable result will be a half-baked answer, which is often worse than none at all. The alternative in the face of limited resources is to limit the study. Pick a topic smaller than world hunger. It doesn't matter how small it is. Success and resource commitment go together. Carry out one effective program in an area of high importance and visibility, and the resources will suddenly appear for more of the same.

3. *Demand value over activity.* This means that the path to value must be established before an activity is undertaken. If you can't find the connection between the internal system, process, policy, or program and an external effect on customers and therefore competitive advantage, then there is probably little value in improving it. In fact, the only sensible thing to do is either radically redesign it so that it can add value or dump it. Activities that are necessary but don't add competitive advantage should be either centralized in a shared service center or outsourced.

Leading the Way Into the Future

The principal shortcoming of best-practice stories is that they focus on yesterday's problems and solutions. You will never get ahead if you practice walking backward into the future. One of the more important sidelights of our study is how the BHAM companies are positioned for the future. The BHAMs are better prepared than most firms to lead the way into the next century because of their focus. Most of The Rest are concentrating on process improvement using a variety of currently popular tools. Common examples are total-quality management (TQM), benchmarking, and reengineering. While it might be a good idea to redesign or reengineer inefficient systems and processes, this practice will not gain you market share in the next millennium. The future will belong to companies that adopt the eight drivers as their modus operandi. That is because these are the fundamental truths of effective management rather than transient fads. The BHAM companies' focus is not on designing twentieth-century processes. It's on inventing twenty-first-century market positions and opportunities.

> **BHAM Lesson:** *Best practice is context, a combination of organizational beliefs, traits, and operating stratagems.*

Building a BHAM Context

Many of the BHAM factors are somewhat intuitive and invisible. To design and build a BHAM context we need to bring the eight factors to the foreground of operational consciousness. This is done most easily by using them as a filter in system design and application. Every time we want to launch a new policy, system, procedure, or program we should ask ourselves how the eight factors can be brought into the design. Figure 1-4 is a checklist for doing this.

Summary

Life is a paradox. From physics to love to organizational management, we are constantly confronted with inconsistencies and incongruities. The search for best practices is one of these contradictions. At one level, it is a waste of time; at another level, it can be very useful. The bad news is that it is seldom done well. The good news is that when it is carried out effectively it can be a great learning experience for everyone involved.

The market is filled with stories of best management practices that are exaggerations, to say the least. In place of well-researched facts, we are given unverifiable, superficial stories. These so-called best practices are nothing more than the visible manifestation of something more basic. Best human asset management is a set of fundamental beliefs, traits, and operating stratagems that constitute the organization's context. They are timeless truths on which institutions are built. They clearly separate the BHAMs from The Rest.

In 1991, the Saratoga Institute's search for best human asset

Figure 1-4. Checklist for generating best-practice drivers.

BEST HUMAN ASSET MANAGEMENT CHECKLIST

VALUE: How will this process/program support the balanced value ethic?

_____

_____

COMMITMENT: What resources do we need to make a long-term commitment to this core strategy?

_____

_____

_____

CULTURE: How does this process/program fit with our culture as it is or as we want it to be?

Fits _____

Needs to Change _____

COMMUNICATION: How will we communicate this: who, which media, what methods?

Who (persons)	Media (e-mail, speech, newsletter, etc.)	Method (personal or group)
_____	_____	_____
_____	_____	_____
_____	_____	_____

PARTNERING: Who from outside our unit must be involved to help drive this program?

_____

_____

COLLABORATION: What role and responsibility will other persons and units in our department have in designing and supporting this process/program?

Person/Unit	Role
_____	_____
_____	_____
_____	_____

INNOVATION AND RISK: What is the risk in this change and how do we reduce it?

_____

_____

_____

COMPETITIVE PASSION: What kind of system will we set up to get constructive feedback on improving this process/program?

_____

_____

management practices within 573 companies led to the discovery of the true nature of "best." Annual follow-up studies involving over 1,000 organizations continue to verify our original findings. The eight best human asset management drivers are: an interwoven human-financial value focus, commitment to a long-term core strategy, linkage of culture and systems, massive multidimensional communications, partnering within and outside the company, collaboration within functional groups, innovation through well-planned and managed risk taking, and a competitive passion that is never satisfied with less than constant improvement.

Investigators have to deal with the chicken or the egg syndrome. Did a practice develop because of the underlying contextual features, or did new features emerge in the context because the practice was successful? We are not in a position to conduct the type of research that would be necessary to support either view. What we do know is that the eight factors are common to The Best and not consistently evident in The Rest. Further support for the efficacy of the eight factors can be found in the financial performance of the BHAMs, which is consistently among the best in their industries.

We have witnessed these factors at work in every successive year of study. Until future investigations produce evidence to the contrary, we believe that these are the distinguishing features of best human asset management. They are also an effective path to market leadership in the twenty-first century.

The chapters that follow detail each factor as a driving force and present case studies of BHAM companies both in the United States and abroad.

References

1. Charles Handy, *The Age of Paradox* (Cambridge, Mass.: Harvard Business School Press, 1994).
2. Winston Churchill, broadcast, October 1, 1939.
3. Jeremy Rifkin, *The End of Work* (New York: Tarcher Putnam, 1995), p. 5.
4. Rifkin, p. 8.

5. William Bridges, *Job Shift* (Reading, Mass.: Addison-Wesley, 1994).
6. Jac Fitz-enz, *Human Value Management* (San Francisco: Jossey-Bass, 1990), p. 10.
7. *Best in America Guidebooks* (Saratoga, Calif.: Saratoga Institute, 1993 and 1994).

2

Balanced Value Fixation

How the Best Put Value Into Every Agenda and Balance the Human and Financial Sides

In the middle of designing a performance measurement system at Prudential Property and Casualty, the vice president of human resources said to me, "I'm sick and tired of hearing, 'What's the value in this?' every time someone suggests a meeting, a project, or changing something." She was joking, because that was precisely what we were trying to persuade everyone to do: Focus on value at all times. As my grandma Emma used to tell me, "Be careful what you pray for, sometimes you get it." Over the next several years, Pru's P & C human resource function proved to be one of the two best-managed of all the companies we studied.

The most notable and ultimately the most important characteristic of the BHAMs is their consistent focus on adding value rather than on merely stimulating activity. Contrary to general belief, being busy is not the same as adding value. Activity is expense. Value is found sometimes in a result. And value is at the heart of BHAMs' visions.

Values along with culture and a long-term commitment to a core strategy make up the structure of a strong company. Of the three, values are the most critical because they drive culture patterns and core strategy formulation. As I mentioned previously, the eight factors are interactive and interrelated. In another way, values, culture, and commitment are the foundation on which are constructed communication systems, partnerships and collaboration, innovation and risk, and a desire for constant improvement. In that sense, values are the keystone of the foundation. Figure 2-1 shows how the BHAM company is structured and how values fit in its framework.

Several Facets of Value

The BHAMs seem to know how to keep all values in sight simultaneously. This isn't easy or everyone would be doing it. Nevertheless, every time a meeting is called, a policy reviewed, an investment contemplated, a system or process designed or redesigned, the issue of the potential gain or loss of value comes up. There is ample evidence that many companies have undertaken reengineering processes that did not add any substantial value. One elementary reason for this is that no one asked the value question at the outset. Everyone simply assumed that there would be value in the change per se. However, because of an absence of con-

Figure 2-1. Best-practice structure.

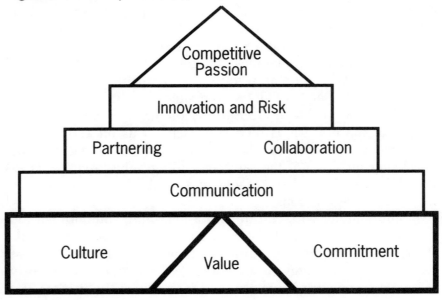

scious understanding of the ultimate competitive advantage that the change might foster, about three out of four change programs fail to improve the position of the company that initiated them. The simple but critical question at the front end of all projects must be, "How will this add value?"

Value can be viewed, assessed, and evaluated from several different angles. These perspectives include:

- ❑ *Type*—human, production, and financial
- ❑ *Location*—within the process or outcome
- ❑ *Focus*—internal or external

Value Types

Human

Human value is the least understood of all. It covers services that prepare people to perform at their best. Production value can be described in terms of positive changes in the company's service, quality, or productivity levels. Financial value is measured in terms of sales, expenses, profits, margins, market share, return on assets or equity, stock price, and the like. The fact is that if we do a good job at adding human value, other things being equal, we improve production values. In turn, these lead ultimately to contributing financial value.

One way of looking at human value is by examining the good things companies do for people. Included here would be benefit programs, training classes, supervisory coaching and mentoring, and personal counseling. These can be evaluated through positive changes in employee attitudes, as measured by surveys, improvement in interpersonal behavior, and overall job performance. One of the tangible payoffs for treating people well is that employees who feel well cared for pass on that attitude to the customers they meet.

SERVICE INDUSTRY SHIFT

Service businesses habitually applied a mass production model in measuring productivity and profits that served them well until the early

1990s. But as customer and employee demographics changed, the model became a curse. It resulted in disaffected customers and low employee morale that translated into high turnover rates. The combination led to flat or falling sales among some of America's leading commercial icons, including Sears and McDonald's. In 1989, 119,000 sales jobs turned over in the Sears Merchandise Group. This cost the company $110 million, 17 percent of the Group's 1989 income.

Companies as different as Marriott and Merck studied the effects of poor morale, high turnover, and customer retention. The results were astounding. Hundreds of millions of dollars were being lost through low productivity, repeated hiring and training costs, disruptions in projects and work relationships. Merck's conclusion was that an investment of 50 percent of an employee's salary in human value activities could reap a payback within one year.

Now, a new paradigm for the service industry is emerging. Leonard Schlesinger and James Heskett have described the effects of this model.[1] It is based on human value. Dayton Hudson, ServiceMaster, Ryder Trucks, and others have rejected the notion that good people are hard to find and that people don't want to work. Top management is investing in people as well as in merchandising. It is employing technology to facilitate work rather than to replace workers. It is truly linking pay and performance, thereby giving low-level employees a chance at earning a living wage. It is supporting the work force with training. In these companies, customers are coming back and sales are on the rise.

Other things being equal, high retention rates and low absenteeism are valid indicators of employees who feel valued. Happy, involved employees obviously enhance the customer's experience with the company. Beyond attitude scores there are more tangible values. At the Mirage Hotel in Las Vegas, top management uses the employee turnover rate as its key human value indicator. In an industry in which turnover averages well over 40 percent the Mirage enjoys an annual average of less than 10 percent. This is because it turns negative aspects of boring jobs into positive reinforcements. Instead of marking down a housekeeper for errors in cleaning a room, Mirage marks up the housekeeper for everything she does right. This gives her positive reinforcement, which in turn leads to the low turnover. This positive attitude toward its people helps Mirage Resorts to be among the most profitable in the industry. There are several ways in which a low turnover rate converts into value for the company.

We've conducted extensive analyses of turnover costs throughout the Americas and consistently found that losing an employee, even a lower-level one, often costs the equivalent of from six months' to one year's pay. Highly skilled technicians, professional specialists, and managers cost as much as twice that to replace. Other studies have estimated turnover costs in the same range. Many of the costs are hidden. Cost is incurred through reduced or lost productivity, hiring expenses, job vacancies, orientation and training expenditures, temporary worker charges, overtime pay, and administrative processing. Perhaps more important, constant turnover adversely affects customer relations. We all feel it when we go to the bank, the grocery story, our favorite restaurant, or other retail establishments we frequently visit. When the staff is changing constantly it is annoying to have to explain our preferences time after time or to build new relationships with service personnel who probably won't be around for long anyway. The result is that we are less likely to be loyal to that organization or to refer business to it.

MASSACHUSETTS MUTUAL LIFE

Every company approaches the value question in its own way. In some it seems to spring from a set of systems or processes. Others build it from a fundamental belief about the relationship of business to personal life. Massachusetts Mutual Life (MML) is a 5,000-employee insurance firm headquartered in Springfield, Massachusetts. Top management there believes that a balance between work and home life is the most effective "contract" to offer employees, if one is looking at the long term. The company's value system calls for creating a work environment designed to accommodate the individual life challenges faced by its people. To support this, MML has created a full range of programs covering work and personal time, dependent care, personal and professional support, and financial assistance. These are played out through flex time, personal time, and alternative work schedules. The underlying belief is that if the people working at MML are able to deal with their personal problems in a timely manner they will be more focused and productive when they are on the job. On the one side, there will be less anxiety and, on the other, the result will be better productivity, quality, and customer service.

At first glance, this management philosophy might appear rather one-sided. Primarily, you see a list of benefits for the worker and some expensive programs for management. But in practice this is not a give-away program. There is a quid pro quo. For instance, if an employee needs time off to handle a personal issue, he or she is expected to make up the time within one week. MML also expects a little extra effort in return for its employee-centered policies, and the company gets it in several ways.

The values accruing to MML from its belief in people are high morale and motivated personnel. These are measurable and correlatable with corporate financial performance. In return for understanding and care, MML employees have an absentee rate almost 25 percent below the industry mean. The turnover rate is 10.2 percent versus 12.8 percent for the life insurance industry as a whole. Considering that turnover costs the company in excess of one year's salary for professionals and managers, a 2.6 percent differential adds up to an annual saving of more than $5 million for MML. That's a net contribution of profits that is the equivalent of booking many new policies. By focusing on the "soft issues," MML has seen productivity, quality, and customer service levels improve, thus confirming the connection between human and financial values.

Production

Production value is the second type of value that companies seek. This can be found in customer service, product quality, or unit cost. The attitude of many people seems to be "action for its own sake." In the hustle and bustle of business it is not uncommon to witness the paradox of people acting without thinking. Businesspeople are constantly urged to action as though that is all that matters. It starts when they walk through the door on Day One and are given their job description. The position document normally is focused on personal background and future *activity*. It states educational, knowledge, and skill requirements, and lists duties and responsibilities.

Job descriptions typically do not deal with the value rationale for creating the position, the tangible values to be generated by the position, or the linkages between or among positions and across functions. They seldom connect the position with its internal suppliers and customers or with the goals of the company. Such a narrowly focused structure leads individuals away from any organizational agendas and concentrates them on being busy. In effect, the position description implies that the employee is to bury his head in the job and not be concerned about what goes on around him.

This might have been okay under the early twentieth-century model of dividing labor and simplifying jobs. But today, when a person is given his job and its objectives by the supervisor, this is supposed to focus him on the company. Moreover, employees are increasingly being assigned to teams. To be effective team players they must know the objectives of the team as well as their own. Unfortunately, as Peter Drucker has pointed out, "Managing by objectives works when we know the objectives, unfortunately we seldom do."[2]

HOLMES REGIONAL MEDICAL CENTER

At Holmes Regional Medical Center in Melbourne, Florida, the job description was reversed and incorporated with its objectives tied directly to the strategic initiatives of the center. The opening lines of the JD read something like this:

> *The purpose of this position is to add value by supporting the four strategic imperatives of HRMC: quality, customer service, employee relations, and fiscal responsibility.*

This immediately connects the employee to the larger values of the enterprise. It focuses attention on the strategic imperatives. Through this unique approach to the position description, Holmes has raised the eyes of the employee from concentrating solely on the task at hand to contributing to the four strategic goals of the company. The job description goes on to state who the suppliers of work for the position are and who the customers of the job outputs are. It also describes the resources that the jobholder is responsible for managing. Then the document shifts to a list of objectives, jointly developed by the supervisor and the employee. Objectives are not random lists of projects. Each person knows which service, quality, or productivity objectives he or she is responsible for achieving. These are set specifically within the four corporate imperatives: quality, customer service, employee relations, and fiscal responsibility. Finally, each objective has quantitative individual and team performance standards. The main benefit of all this is that everyone knows how they are personally contributing to the success of HRMC. This generates job satisfaction. It also has helped the company become extremely cost-effective as well as one of the highest-rated medical centers in terms of patient satisfaction.

Financial

When an organization does a good job of building human and production values it is naturally rewarded with financial value. The BHAMs understand this three-step value path. Production costs go down, sales go up, customers return time and again, margins improve, market share grows, and returns on assets and equity improve. In the long run, they prosper more consistently than The Rest, which simply aim to make as much money as they can. The reason for the long-term prosperity of the BHAMs is that they have a value foundation that carries them through the rough times that fall on every organization sooner or later.

Value Measurement

Value can be measured through a combination of five indices of change: cost, time, quantity, error rate, and human reaction. These can be applied to the three value types, which can be condensed into service, quality, and productivity. Figure 2-2 shows examples of these values indices.

Typically, cost is a productivity measure: cost per unit of product or service. It can also be used in quality: cost of nonconformance (involving rework or customer complaints). Time is used by the quality people: cycle time of a process. Volume is a productivity measure: ratio of inputs to outputs. Error rate is obviously qual-

Figure 2-2. Value measurement path.

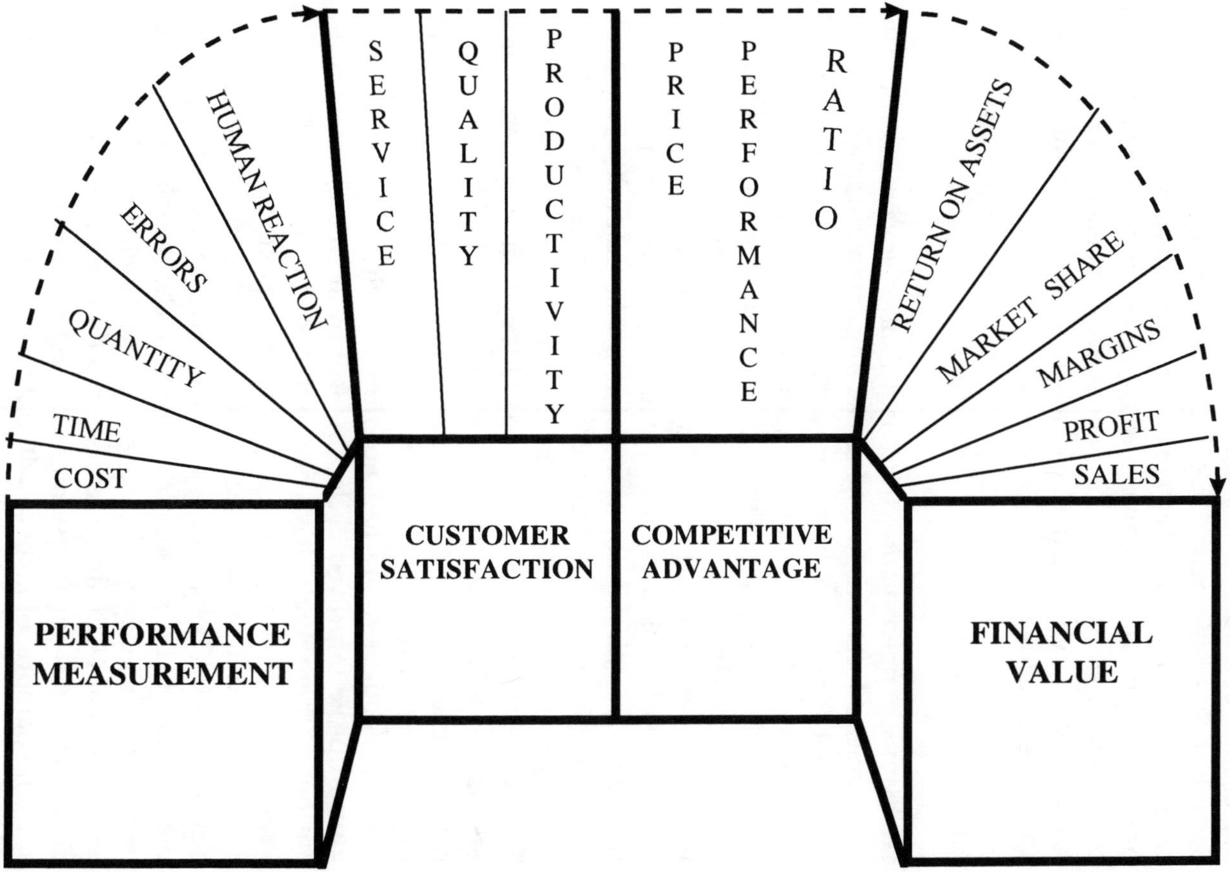

ity. Human reaction is a service measure, as in customer satisfaction or employee morale.

Once these apparent value improvements have been identified they must pass through the customer filter. Here is where *evaluation* takes place. It is customers who rule on value. If they say they are satisfied, you are on your way to acquiring a competitive advantage. When you do that you are rewarded with the financial values listed above.

Value Location

As I've mentioned before, there is a fixation on process in many companies. Most managers when reading about the latest improvement tool forget that there are differences among the tool, the problem, and the solution. Reengineering, quality methods, and benchmarking are process tools. They are neither the problem nor the solution, any more than a hammer can build a house all by itself. The natural outgrowth of this process fixation is the neglect of the essential objective, which is to add value. This disregard for the obvious is played out by managers who commit resources to improving a process without connecting it to a stated ultimate value. Just improving cycle time does not necessarily add value. TransCanada Pipe Line was able to reduce the time needed to process a sales document from twelve days to four. When it proudly told its customers about this, the response was, "Who cares?" The apparent improvement in internal cycle time meant nothing to the customer and therefore had no intrinsic value. If TCPL had followed up the improved cycle time feature with the benefit to the customer, there might have been interest. Therein lies the point. Improved features are not always customer benefits.

I am almost embarrassed to point out that when we improve a process the real objective is to create a competitive advantage for the company in the marketplace. This is such a simplistic statement that the reader may scoff at my even mentioning it. However, as exemplified at TCPL and a few thousand other places, process improvement does not always mean market value.

The paradox of activity without value lives. How do you kill it? Look at what the BHAMs do. They ask the prime question, "What is the value in doing this?" Could it be any simpler or truer?

In science everyone agrees that the most elegant solution is the simplest. $E = mc^2$ is the classic example. This most important discovery in physics since Isaac Newton discovered gravity is expressed in just three variables. Unfortunately, businesspeople don't seem to subscribe to science's dictum. Often executives will engage consulting firms to carry out massive, time-consuming, and extremely expensive analyses when the solution is as simple as a couple of bright people sitting down and together running through a logic chain.

We ran into a case like this with a client who had a very time-consuming staffing process. On average, it took this company seven weeks longer to fill key jobs than their competitors took. In situations like this reengineering processes are often the hammer that executives employ. The project can take weeks and cost thousands of dollars. Yet a simple examination of the steps in this case showed that there was a chain of fifteen approval signatures that had to be obtained to start the sourcing process. Yes, that's right, fifteen! As with many cases we've seen, some process just builds up over time and no one notices until it becomes outrageous. Research revealed that in this case, after the first approver signed off, so did everyone else. Fourteen wasted signatures. The solution was simple. With the stroke of a pen the company changed its policy. It went to two signatures and saved six weeks in process time.

Perhaps it is a belief that bigger is better that causes executives to spend millions to solve simple problems. I remember someone describing Peter Drucker's style of consulting: "He comes in, sits down, listens to the issues, asks a few questions, provides a profound but simple solution and leaves." I guess when one is a good analyst one doesn't need an army of MBAs running prepackaged solutions for six months.

Value Focus

The internal versus the external look at potential value is largely another way of describing the process versus the outcome value. We can make improvements in our internal departmental processes and stop there. For example, a change in strategy, policy, or work flow can substantially improve the outcome of one of our processes. It could shorten the time needed to fill jobs, cut paychecks, process invoices, get ad copy to the printer, print out and distribute a monthly report, or generate a purchase order. The question is, "So what?" What is the value in doing that? Does this output represent a valuable input to the customer's process? One department's output is another department's input. If I can provide you with any one of the above outputs, what value is that to you? To locate actual customer value there may be several iterations of this question as each unit's output becomes the next unit's input until ultimately the company output lands in the hands of the external customer—the one who gives us money for our product or service. In every marketplace since the beginning of caveman bartering, the customer has been the final arbiter of value.

I could give you case after case of this sequential input-output process, but I think you have grasped the idea by now. What separates the BHAMs from the pack is that they run out the value chain *before* they commit the resources. That is one of the main reasons why they are among the most successful and profitable companies over the long term.

The Need for a Vision and Values

Every organization from the nuclear family up to the megacorporation has a vision that encompasses a set of values. Nearly every new management book features a section on corporate values. Sometimes these belief systems exist mainly at the subconscious level. At others they are trumpeted constantly in the form of the company vision. Values have always been at the core of any group endeavor. As far back as the Bible we read:

> *Where there is no vision, the people perish.*
> —Proverbs 29:18

Most research on leadership has revealed vision as a defining factor. John P. Kotter points out what research has consistently found, that the first thing successful leaders do is to provide a vision for people to rally around.[3] His research has shown that leaders offer "a vision of what should be, a vision which takes into account the legitimate interests of all the people involved." Offering a vision is the key difference between managing and leading. Managers administer policies and systems; leaders inspire with a vision. Some people bemoan things as they are. Leaders see things as they are and then describe what they could be.

Values drive decisions. They become the foundation of the culture and as such contribute to the design of operating and administrative systems. They are at the heart of management philosophies. A simple example is the policy a company has regarding employee access to supplies. Executives with authoritarian values that imply a lack of trust in others bar employees from the supply room. Sometimes they install control systems that cost more than any reasonable loss of supplies through pilferage would entail. Humanistic values assume that people are essentially honest, so managers of this stripe allow employees direct access to supplies. The proven assumption is that any minor losses will be more than offset by improved productivity and mutual trust. I'm not a Pollyanna who believes unquestionably in the goodness of all people. There is at least one exception to this rule that should be noted: If you are operating in a region where most of the people live below the poverty level, it is probably not wise to leave the supply room open.

Beyond Profit

Historically, a few visionary business leaders have espoused humanistic as well as commercial values. Yet a true appreciation of and support for humanistic values are relatively rare, public statements notwithstanding. For many profit-making organizations, the discussion of values is a recent event.

I recall vividly trying to talk with my bosses and peers in the 1960s and 1970s about a "philosophy" of management. I was warned not to use the word because it smacked of softness and fuzzy thinking, whereas business was about pragmatism. Fortunately, that famous folk philosopher Bob Dylan was right when he proclaimed, "The times they are a-changin'." Many people, including business managers, have come to realize that there is something very fundamental about business that is beyond the pursuit of profit. Management guru Peter Drucker has enlightened us in many ways regarding the nature of organizations and the role of management. Statements such as "the purpose of a business is to create a customer" lead us to appreciate that creating value for someone else in turn generates values for ourselves.

The citizenry of the United States enjoyed unprecedented prosperity for about thirty years following World War II. As that era drew to an end in the 1980s, people realized that money didn't necessarily mean happiness and peace of mind—even though it is probably better to be miserable and rich than miserable and poor. In the 1990s the arguments of the environmentally concerned began to take on added credibility. Value assumed more than an economic color. The egocentric greed cult of the 1980s self-destructed over the notion that business was only about making money.

Some companies have espoused and practiced a dual value philosophy for decades. Some endured ridicule for it. Just before World War I, Henry Ford raised the wages of his factory workers to $5 a day, almost double the pay rate for the times. He did it for two reasons: to improve the lives of his workers (idealism) and to give them the money they would need one day to buy an automobile (pragmatism). Yet Ford's apparently altruistic statements at the time were reviled by some as interjecting ethical issues into business, where they were clearly out of place.

More recently, other farsighted leaders of industry have made similar commitments. Examples are evident in companies that have been highly successful for decades. Hewlett Packard, Motorola, Merck, Xerox, and Federal Express are just a few of the more prominent ones. Nevertheless, altruistic values are not a guarantee of success. They have appeared and then been swallowed up in such short-lived success stories as that of People's Express. We've also seen them in great firms like Control Data, which floundered after periods of humanistic leadership. Humanism by itself is no replacement for good business sense, but when combined, the two are a highly synergetic force.

Value Dualism

Because the BHAMs focus on adding value at all times, they see simultaneously the two sides of value: financial and humanistic.

Time after time, we have found examples of managers working with employees to capture both values.

The Asten Group, Inc., a Charleston, South Carolina, manufacturer of industrial fabrics, exemplifies this trend. Asten's management was determined to improve the safety record of the company. To accomplish this it charged a group of supervisors and managers with developing a safety program that would have a gain-sharing feature within it. The group responded by designing Team$hare. This program puts safety in the hands of the workers, who can benefit in two ways from reducing accidents. The first benefit is that fewer people are hurt on the job. The second is that, as accident rates and worker compensation costs decline, the people share in the savings.

The proposal fit Asten's values and culture, which are based on a belief in treating people with respect and giving them *real* responsibility that goes beyond what their job descriptions set forth. In addition to its formal benefits, Team$hare helps workers understand that safety is important and that it is *their* business. An additional positive side effect is that as the workers are trained in the features of the gain-sharing plan they learn how incentive compensation programs are structured and funded. This gives them a greater appreciation for all the intricate considerations that go into paying people.

The Asten case is a small, isolated example of dualistic values. Nevertheless, our research has shown consistently that success is based on fundamental principles played out in thousands of small as well as large policies, programs, and processes. In our experience, we see that if you do the thousands of small things well you achieve the few big things that make the difference. And if you don't do the little things, your only hope is to be damned lucky.

A VALUES-DRIVEN COMPANY

The Iams Company is one of the best examples of a value fixation. It provides a unique angle on the balanced value operation. Iams is a maker of premium pet foods, with four plants in Ohio and its headquarters in Dayton. Every year it has qualified as a best-practice company. Over the past decade it has increased its market share steadily.

At the base of this superb performance is Iams's dual value belief system. It starts with a compensation policy that pays above the industry average and rewards employees according to a combination of personal performance and corporate results. So far, this is not all that extraordinary. What makes Iams different, and more successful than other companies that pay the same way, is that Iams developed and maintains a full support system underneath the compensation plan. The company uses what it calls a productivity incentive plan (PIP) in concert with a certification program for production workers.

First, the PIP covers all employees. It is composed of base pay plus incentives for meeting or exceeding sales, profit, and return on invested capital goals. This structure is in turn supported by an intensive employee communications program. Plant performance on a variety of operating factors is monitored and displayed daily for all employees to see. The CEO is very visible in the company. He visits operating units to chat with the people individually and in small groups. His behavior models the Iams belief statement, which reads "Employees are essential to our success and we will provide opportunities for job challenges, training, and self-development."

Early in each calendar quarter, employees are assembled to review the results of the past quarter. It is important to note that the CEO personally presents these results. The motivating power of the boss speaking directly to employees is not to be ignored. Everyone sees that it is important to achieve business goals and also that the leadership has a very sincere regard for the people who make it happen.

The second feature of the Iams people and profits program is the certification program. Production employees move from job to job for the purpose of cross-training. When they finish and demonstrate their new, expanded capabilities, they are certified on the basis of the knowledge and skills they have acquired. Future merit pay increases are based in part on certification. An important feature that undoubtedly contributes to its success is that the program is monitored continually by a team of supervisors and employees. This further shows the company's faith in its people.

When the original plan was designed, the human resources managers and supervisors met with every hourly employee to make sure each one understood the plan. Even with this level of personal attention, initially there was apprehension among some of the employees. To overcome it, the human resources staff held counseling sessions with anxious employees and listened to their concerns. They explained the details of the program again and assured employees that the plan could be modified should it be shown to be unfair or unworkable.

Considering the time expenditure and probable cost of such follow-through, one might think that written memos and group meetings could accomplish the same result. Perhaps this is so, but probably not. The history of failed improvement programs fairly screams with evidence that indicts management groups that weren't willing to become personally involved. Common sense tells us that the comprehension and motivation gained by employees from personal meetings are quantum leaps higher than what typically results from group meetings.

The distinguishing features of presidential involvement, personal meetings, and employee-supervisor program management are what make Iams's systems so effective. Iams is one of the best of many examples in which attention to detail and going the extra mile contributed to exceptional performance. The lesson is an old one. Doing something right the first time yields extraordinary results. It also eliminates the frustration, anger, waste, and disillusion that come from having to do it over because the program didn't work the first time around.

One can argue with methodology. The specific applications that work so well for Iams may not, probably will not, work well for everyone. That is exactly the point made in Chapter 1. The application, program, system, or process is not the point. Best practice is the combination and interaction of values, commitment, culture, and so on that drove the design and implementation of the applications. In turn, this caused Iams to excel in productivity, quality, and service. Iams's productivity is among the highest in the industry. The PIP and certification program are the visible drivers that pushed productivity up over 10 percent in the early 1990s with no increased capital investment. Even though Iams pays above the mean for its industry, its payroll, as a percent of revenue, in the 1992–95 period was 8.6 percent versus the industry average of 16.5 percent. That is a competitive advantage that any CEO could love.

The Challenge

It's not always easy to refute the paradox that claims you either make money or make people happy. Many of us have been raised with this apparent contradiction staring us down. Logic, as we've been told, shows that you can't have your cake and eat it too. Western philosophy is based on Aristotle's laws of logic. His second law is that a thing is either A or not A, the law of the excluded middle. It would follow then that if you want to make money you must be hard on people. The management corollary is that if you are nice to people they will take advantage of you. And experience proves that this is true—for about 5 percent or less of the working population. That is the Theory X notion that Douglas McGregor described in the 1960s. But he went on to point out that the remaining 95 percent of the work force are well-meaning, motivated people who take pride in their work and arrive at work wanting to do well. This is McGregor's Theory Y view.

Business magazines periodically feature "America's Toughest Bosses" articles, apparently under the impression that toughness is something to be emulated. Have you ever seen a feature on America's wisest bosses? Folklore offers a lesson that the BHAM companies have taken to heart. It is, "What you put out is what you get back." Because of the 5 percent whose personal insecurities cause them to be counterproductive, some of us are tempted to treat the other 95 percent as impersonal economic units. Our challenge is to keep the 5 percent to 95 percent ratio in mind no matter what a small minority does. Building consistently from a foundation of people *and* profits rather than people *or* profits typically produces a positive reaction from the 95 percent.

In *Built to Last*, James C. Collins and Jerry I. Porras state:

> *"[W]e did not find maximizing shareholder wealth or profit maximization as the dominant driving force or primary objective through the history of the visionary companies."*[4]

In seventeen out of eighteen pairs of companies they studied, their visionary companies were more ideologically driven and less purely profit-driven than the corresponding company. In every case, the ideological company's long-term profitability exceeded that of its comparison company.

One of the best examples of the payoff for this management philosophy is the Hewlett-Packard Company. The founders, Bill

Hewlett and Dave Packard, believed their company should be managed first and foremost to make a contribution to society. A competitor, Texas Instruments, offers an opposite example. In that organization the strategy was simply to grow the company as large as possible. Unfortunately for TI, the obsession with growth for its own sake left the company far behind H-P in total sales. In 1995, their Fortune 500 revenues and ranks were:

Hewlett-Packard:	$31.6B—20th
Texas Instruments:	$13.1B—89th

Growth for its own sake should not be the objective. Growth profitability and stakeholder value are the natural rewards for developing a valid and effective operating strategy and executing it efficiently. In effect, these indices are merely the scorecard. If we choose to do the things that suit the market, and if we do them better than most of our competitors, we will grow and create more value.

Words vs. Actions

Anyone can print a statement of values or purpose and broadcast it far and wide. This is a common habit of insincere, naive, or lazy managers. It's much more difficult to live the statement. This is the difference between the BHAM companies and The Rest.

MICROGRAFX

Micrografx was founded in 1982 to develop graphic software applications. It employs 300 people in Dallas. To help contain health care costs as well as to provide an opportunity for employees to enjoy better health, management funded a fitness center. Being a small company made this investment somewhat risky. Still, the company felt the benefits outweighed the cost. From the beginning, employees were deeply involved in the fitness scheduling and management of the program. Employees can use the fitness center at any time during the workday. Management trusts them.

Micrografx management didn't limit its concern for employees to the fitness center. Since most employees sit at computers all day, their necks and shoulders often become stiff and tense. Looking ahead, management provided a masseuse at a nominal cost to work out neck and shoulder tension. Extensive communication on wellness topics, child care, parenting skills, investments, and tax tips is ongoing. Family members as well as employees are welcome to view these topics on videotapes. Micrografx executives realize that the knowledge and support of the family are also very important.

The Micrografx culture is based on a working partnership with employees in support of values related to the whole person. The company is committed to a long-term program of employee support and respect. Communications are totally open, with bottom-to-top communication strongly encouraged. The result of this humanistic and pragmatic management is an above-average financial performance.

Contradictory Evidence

I have stated repeatedly that in many organizations what is actually valued is activity rather than results. I can make this outrageous statement simply because I have witnessed it countless times. Look at the opposite side of my claim. If you wanted people to produce value-adding results, how would you train, manage, and reward them? I suggest that you would do something like the following:

1. Train your people in analytic skills.
2. Encourage them to understand the problem or opportunity before firing a solution at it.
3. Set up recognition systems, starting with base and incentive pay, that would reward employees for adding tangible value rather than for merely completing an activity.
4. Truly differentiate pay and other forms of recognition between the top, middle, and low performers.
5. Withhold rewards from, counsel, retrain, or terminate those who do not perform according to the twin human/financial value goals.

Very few—that is, an exceedingly small number of companies—do these five things. In the first case, fewer than 10 percent of the companies we've surveyed or worked with build analytic skills even though it is indisputable that our school system does not teach people to think. Check your training curriculum for courses on operational or administrative analysis.

Most companies encourage action. Some even support risk taking. But only a few demand that their people grasp the implications of a problem before they blast off in a quest for the holy grail of solutions. Instead, the unspoken but clearly accepted cultural mandate is "Do *something*."

Most organizations have some type of objective-setting system. Examination of the objectives usually discloses that the goal is to complete a project but not necessarily to show evidence of its effects. This is the smoking gun that proves activity is the goal. It is what Drucker means when he claims that we seldom know the true and final objective of adding value. That is different from intermediate program goals.

The fourth and most obvious missing link is differential rewards. If we are honest, we will admit that in most companies the take-home pay of performers in the top third is only marginally higher than that received by the bottom third in any job grade level. Employees aren't stupid. They see that exceptional performance and exceptional pay are not common corollaries. What we sow is what we reap.

Finally, to top it off, many managers tolerate disruptive and contrary behavior far too long. Instead of jumping on it early with proper counseling, support, and warnings, they let it fester and infect other employees. When asked what he would do with a high performer who did not live the culture of General Electric, CEO Jack Welch claims he would fire that person.

A True Short Story

Even the best-known companies ignore several of these principles. In the midst of a benchmarking project at one of the Baldrige Award winners, I was talking with a manager when her secretary brought in an envelope. She excused herself and opened it. Then, with an amused look, she turned to me and said, "This is my annual performance bonus check. I haven't any idea what I got this for." And she was the compensation manager! I swear this is true because I wouldn't have the guts to make up such an outrageous story.

As you study the balanced value fixation it becomes clear that it influences the development and maintenance of the culture. Time and again, as you will see, value and culture are closely linked elements in the best human asset management companies.

BHAM Lesson: *Always ask, "What is the value in doing this?"*

How to Build a Balanced Value Fixation

It's easy to talk about value, values, vision, mission, and other such abstractions. It's quite another thing to develop them and live by them through thick and thin. The key criterion in values is not quantity but quality. In fact, the more values a company claims to have, the harder it is to live up to them. Experience shows that there is an inverse correlation between the number of words in a vision, mission, or values statement and the amount of truth in it. How does your corporate value system look? Figure 2-3 lists a series of questions you can use to raise the topic and work on it.

Give this questionnaire to any group. It is most interesting to start at the top with the senior management team and see how much agreement there is in the answers given. Do these people all list the same values? If not, what are the implications for strategizing and working together? As you move down the organizational ladder and try it on lower levels, what do you see? Do first-line supervisors see company values the same way that top management does? If not, what difference do you think this will make?

Summary

An obsession with value is one of the most obvious and pervasive hallmarks of BHAM companies. They do what The Rest only talk about.

Figure 2-3. Corporate values questionnaire.

1. Our company exhibits a strong value orientation.

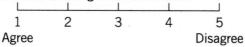

    1   2   3   4   5
  Agree   Disagree

2. We can see value being applied as a criterion in almost everything we do.

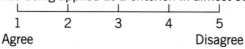

    1   2   3   4   5
  Agree   Disagree

3. When it comes to competing human and financial values, management does a good job of balancing them.

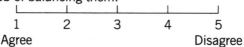

    1   2   3   4   5
  Agree   Disagree

4. The most fundamental values that we adhere to as a company are:

   a. _____

   b. _____

   c. _____

   d. _____

   e. _____

5. The most fundamental purpose behind our company's existence now and for the next 100 years is:

_____

_____

(maximum of 10 words)

Values can be viewed from several angles. Human values include security and opportunities for growth. Production values encompass quality, service, and productivity. Financial values are expressed in sales, market share, return on equity, and so forth. All measures of value come back to the fact that the customer makes the final decision about the value of a company's outputs.

The key trait among the BHAM companies is their dualistic view of value. First, they are obsessively focused on adding value in everything they do. Second, they believe and practice the concept of balancing human and financial values. They have shown over the decades that a company can be humane as well as profitable.

Activity does not always equate with value added. By definition, activity is expense. Results have potential value if they connect with competitive advantage. An action that improves the internal process or outcome is not always valued by the external customer. The lesson is clear. Start on the outside. Learn what the customer values the most. Then, look inside and see which processes, policies, or strategies need to be modified or improved to generate the value sought by the customer.

Finally, live the values. Words engraved on plaques and printed on wallet cards are good reminders, but they are not sufficient to create a value culture. The map is not the territory. It's one thing to say it. It's quite another to live it through thick and thin. The winners are the ones who commit themselves to the value path and stay on it no matter how much it hurts. Ultimately, they prosper because they have a sound foundation on which to survive the tough times and exploit the good times.

References

1. Leonard Schlesinger and James Heskett, "The Service Driven Service Company," *Harvard Business Review*, September–October 1991, pp. 71–81.
2. Peter Drucker, cover quotation, *Management Review*, November 1995.
3. John P. Kotter, *The Leadership Factor* (New York: The Free Press, 1988).
4. James C. Collins and Jerry I. Porras, *Built to Last* (New York: HarperCollins, 1994).

3

Commitment
to a Core Strategy

*How the Best Generate
and Sustain Long-Term
Commitment to a Basic Strategy
That Builds an Institution*

In 1981, Motorola acquired the computer company in which I was vice president of industrial relations. One night during a joint management dinner, Robert Galvin, then chairman of Motorola, told me what he went through to change the culture of the company. Early in the 1970s he had recognized that Motorola's paternalism had to give way to a participative culture. The complexity of products, the emerging competition, and the speed of change were so apparent to him that he launched the culture change effort. Despite the full, driving weight of his office and his position as son of the founder, he said it took about eight years to move most managers from the old to the new culture. That is the best example of long-term commitment to a core strategy I have ever heard of or seen.

Books on strategic planning often give short shrift to the issue of commitment. Instead, they focus on the processes within strategic organizational planning. They point out that it is important to link the corporate strategic plan to the local business units through a series of cascading objectives. So far as this goes, it is correct. But they are deficient when it comes to two points. One is that before there can be a strategic plan there has to be a core strategy. The second is management commitment. The BHAMs are notable for their statement of and long-term commitment to a core strategy.

In *The Discipline of Market Leaders*, Michael Treacy and Fred Wiersema argue for a commitment to one of three core strategies.[1] They label them value disciplines. One is *operational excellence*. This produces standard products at the best price with the least inconvenience for the customer. Wal-Mart is the model. Another discipline is *product leadership*. Here the emphasis is on product performance enhanced by continual innovation. Their example is Nike. The third value discipline is *customer intimacy*. This is a focus on giving each and every customer exactly what they value. Nordstrom in retailing and Cable and Wireless in telecommunications are featured.

According to the authors, the key element that makes a value discipline effective is total commitment:

> *"A value discipline can't be grafted onto or integrated into a company's normal operating philosophy. It is not a marketing plan, a public relations campaign, or a way to chat up stockholders. The selection is a central act that shapes every subsequent plan and decision a company makes, coloring the entire organization, from its competencies to its culture. The choice of value discipline, in effect, defines what a company does and therefore what it is."*[2]

Strategists show a tendency to ignore the irrefutable fact that nothing gets done, especially in times of adversity, unless there is human commitment to it. In fact, much of business modeling is sterile in its avoidance of the human involvement and consequences. Those who adopt that mechanical attitude end up paying a heavy price. The most dramatic example is reengineering.

According to all reports, 70 percent of the early reengineering projects were unmitigated disasters because they ignored the psychological effect of asking people to give up everything they knew and start over. How could they have expected employees to joyfully support an idea that took away everything they knew and had worked for? Management systems are not active entities. They are inert. Only when human beings commit themselves to supporting the core strategy and building the appropriate systems do we find success. The 1980s management model showed us the long-term costs of financial manipulation in place of commitment to core strategy and value.

Strategic Planning and Long-Term Commitment

In the first year of our research we identified two related best human asset management practices: strategic planning and long-term commitment. By the second year it had become apparent that the distinguishing feature of the BHAMs was that they integrated the two. Almost every organization has some form of strategic plan. Too few organizations exhibit the commitment to make strategies work.

BHAM companies make a long-term commitment to a basic strategy (e.g., shifting the culture to participative, operating ethically, providing the best service in the world, producing or marketing based on the lowest price, or turning out the top-quality product). A strategy should always be stated in the superlative tense. Why just aim to be better? Once the commitment is made, strategic and tactical plans can be developed. Plans change yearly or more often. Strategies endure. A plan is like making a reservation for a dinner date on a Saturday night. A commitment is like getting married for life. The issue is not a plan, it is making the commitment.

Many plans are like wallpaper—pretty but not very strong on their own. Strategic plans must be laid on a core strategy, a solid wall of values. A strategic business plan should be like an architectural drawing. Architects start with a purpose: a building of some type. Before they put pencil to paper they have to agree with whomever is involved that this will be a commercial building designed to optimize some type of function. If they are working for a developer who is building on spec, then the resulting plan will be for general use. It works for developers but not for corporate managers, who must have some fundamental issues clearly agreed upon before they commit themselves to planning.

One of the reasons that some strategic plans don't work is that they are nothing but paper. This is the SOS method of planning. It stands for Strategy on the Shelf. The plan is painstakingly drawn up and then put on the shelf for reference in case of a crisis. However, everyone knows that when the first storm hits, the paper will be torn away because there is no central solid core to which it is attached. So, let's admit one fundamental seldom-spoken truth. It's a heckuva lot easier to draw up a plan than it is to convince people to use it and be true to it. The corollary is, without human commitment, all you have is pretty wallpaper.

Where commitment is present, strategic plans jump out of the files and come to life. Core strategies lead to strategic plans, organizational charts, operating plans, quantitative objectives, and, ultimately, to specific human behavior and task performance. A marked difference between the BHAMs and The Rest appears after plans are developed and implementation has begun. At the first sign of ambiguity or unforeseen occurrences, The Rest quickly drop down from the strategic level and fire off a series of often short-lived, irrelevant actions. We call this the program *du jour* strategy school, illustrated in Figure 3-1. Yesterday they jumped on the quality bandwagon. Today it's benchmarking, tomorrow it may be reengineering, and God only knows what they will do next week. If no new management fads appear in the bookstores, they may soon have no clue as to where to turn next.

There is nothing inherently wrong with applying any of these widely advertised process management tools. The point is that tools have specific uses. They are not panaceas for every evil that springs from Pandora's box. The program *du jour* M.O. is an example of the baby and the hammer syndrome. Given a new hammer, the baby goes about indiscriminately beating on everything just for the sheer joy of the pounding. The BHAMs don't do this. They hold to values and long-term goals while reacting to change in ways that keep them moving in pursuit of that dream. The companies that have long-term success records spend their resources in building something of lasting value rather than in just trying to win today's game.

One of the commonest cries these days is, "I don't have enough time." It's true for The Rest because they quickly forget their vision and goals. When faced with an unexpected change,

key suggestion coming out of the task force was to give managers the authority to reward superior performance on the part of both individuals and teams. Step one required top management and human resources to relinquish some control and transfer it into the hands of field managers.

Over the first eighteen months all plans in the field and the office, including one for hourly personnel, were redesigned. This last point is not to be overlooked. Often sales and service professionals are given new plans while the support staff is ignored. One of the many subtle characteristics of BHAM companies is that *everyone* is considered a value-adding associate.

The follow-up step was to develop CVS's new Integrated Management Performance System. It was composed of the following:

1. Individual performance expectations (goal planning)
2. Continuous performance evaluation and feedback (results management)
3. Performance recognition (monetary and nonmonetary rewards)
4. Individual development planning (career pathing)
5. Organization/succession planning (mobilizing for the future)

Note that this is another example of how BHAM companies build support systems behind their strategies. They go past hyperbole and back their words with employee-manager–developed plans and processes. Usually these plans and processes are run by or monitored by cross-functional teams.

At the beginning of each plan year, the CEO's top team sets the corporate objectives for that year. These cascade down through the business units to the team and individual objective level. All objectives are measurable and quantifiable in terms of value-adding results. All objectives are reviewed twice a year and performances rated. A performance review board supports the system to ensure consistency. It looks for linkages among the cascading objectives. The board meets with each department head annually to evaluate the effectiveness of their performance management process. This is another living example of commitment, since senior managers are involved on this board. They didn't underwrite the new system and then walk away. They demonstrated their personal commitment through their involvement.

Extensive, ongoing communications and training underpin the program. All employees are informed in detail about the workings of the program, and a human resources professional is assigned to each department. The job of human resources is to help employees understand the complexities of the process and allay any fears they might have. HR continues to work with the supervisors, supporting their efforts with teams and individuals. Central communications take many forms, including a quarterly newsletter from the president, which can include letters of appreciation and lists of awards as well as comments from the president.

Based on the task force recommendations, a performance recognition program was developed. Different areas and stores formed committees that tailored the program to fit their particular circumstances. This made the system theirs and not management's. Thus, commitment is built at the lowest levels. Recognition is multifaceted, ranging from annual, formal recognitions of outstanding managers and pharmacists to the informal "recognition cards" that senior executives can hand out when visiting stores. The idea is to *catch an employee doing something right* and reward her on the spot. Each card has an associated prize. The magnitude or value of the prize is secondary. Personal recognition is the key motivator.

The continuous, visible dedication of senior management shows the staff the commitment the company is putting into the new system. This is a large part of the success of the new compensation drivers. Management walks its talk.

Commitment to the Future

Lest we fall prey to looking only at the past here, I'd like to turn your attention to what's coming over the horizon. One of the hot items in the mid-1990s is competence. The work of David McClellan at Harvard in the 1960s and 1970s on achievement motivation and competency assessment provided the early basis for today's competency models.[3] Currently, executives are searching for a response to the new drivers emerging with the approach of the third millennium A.D. Some of them have come to the realization that the future is very unpredictable. Others realize that the program *du jour* is counterproductive. Therefore, the wiser among them have drilled to bedrock for something that will always be required for organizational performance. That something, they've concluded, is employee competence. This conclusion is being built into the strategic plans of many BHAM companies. It is taking various forms, but in all cases an attempt is being made to make competency development one of the cornerstones of the strategic commitment.

There are semantic arguments about the differences between the terms *competence* and *skill*. Lyle Spencer and Signe Spencer consider skills and knowledge as surface elements of competence, and belief systems and motives as the core competencies.[4] Thus, competence is a complex set of skills that covers a range of invisible traits and visible capabilities. An organization may choose to work on the core or on the surface competencies.

An example of a comprehensive yet simple approach is that taken by Motorola. This company drives all human development around three factors:

1. Business and technical knowledge/skill: the basic skills of an electronics company
2. Relationship management: interpersonal proficiency
3. Conceptual thinking: the ability to analyze and solve problems

Motorola refers to these as its core human competencies. Many companies confuse competencies, as they call them, with specific job skills. It is very difficult to develop a corporate commitment to a multitude of surface task skills. Skill requirements follow technology or market changes. Yesterday's skill needs will not necessarily be the same as tomorrow's. By taking a more basic approach, Motorola is building competencies that will never go out of style.

COMMITMENT TO COMPETENCE: AMES RUBBER

Ames Rubber Company operates four plants in New Jersey that manufacture imaging rollers for photocopying machines and rubber seals used in automobiles. Through the late 1980s, Ames's business cycle was quite erratic. Because of an unpredictable order pattern, Ames resorted to hiring a large number of temporary workers from a variety of sources. As orders came in, the company staffed up to meet demand; then, as the order rate slowed, Ames laid off people.

This cyclical process created several problems. First, it was distracting, demotivating, and expensive. Involuntary turnover was 59 percent between 1987 and 1989. The revolving door created stress among the permanent staff, with voluntary turnover among full-time employees reaching 38 percent! Second, the company's major customer, Xerox, was complaining about the quality of the rollers Ames was turning out. Clearly, drastic action was called for. There had to be a rethinking of and fundamental changes in the way the company saw itself, its customers, and its employees.

Ames's initial effort followed the typical path—it was a process response. The company invested in better equipment and launched process improvement programs. But as with most such approaches, they didn't improve anything. In retrospect, management realized that its attack had been fragmented, that it lacked a coherent strategy, uniform approaches to problem solving, and a clear understanding of what Ames needed to do to serve customer requirements. As I pointed out earlier, changing a process is not an improvement if the customer doesn't value the result.

Based on a knowledge of why it had failed, Ames regrouped. First, the company formed a strategy review committee comprised of members of the executive committee plus key managers. They studied their chief customer, Xerox, and its approach to quality improvement. Using the Xerox quality leadership model, they started over. One of the first actions was to actively involve top management. There was a commitment to putting top management right in the middle of the improvement program. The new program materials, read by everyone, stated:

> *"Management behavior is the single most important factor in communicating the Total Quality Process. The company's senior executives must make an uncompromising commitment to implement Total Quality and personally involve themselves in the effort."*

This stated commitment took on life when each executive became personally responsible for presenting one aspect of the TQM process. This direct, hands-on engagement of the CEO, the executive committee, and other senior executives was later recognized as the driver that got the program accepted and committed to by the employees.

Early on, a study of the turnover problem uncovered a correlation between turnover rates and quality. Not surprisingly, as turnover went down, yield rates went up. This provided evidence that a new set of values regarding people was imperative. In place of the revolving door practice of frequent binge hiring followed by layoffs, a different strategy emerged. The new plan was to hire and retain a carefully selected and well-trained (or competent) permanent work force. This took the place of an employment strategy that had been based on contingent workers.

New strategy required new data. A review of the people who had voluntarily left showed that a particular type of individual didn't like working at Ames and therefore could be considered a high-risk hire. A plan to improve retention by involving line managers in hiring was developed. At first, the professional human resources staff wasn't too keen on letting go. But by training supervisors in interviewing techniques and by providing support from the professional staff, HR personnel saw that the line managers could do the job previously reserved for them.

The payoffs for Ames's commitment to a new way of working have been dramatic. Absenteeism costs have been more than halved over the past three years. Accident rates are down from twelve to four days per employee. Grievances dropped by two-thirds during this period. Naturally, quality improved. Defects dropped from 30,000 per million parts to just 11! Sales per employee rose from $78,200 to $194,400 in four years. And Ames topped it off by winning the Baldrige Award in 1993. All this took place with a smaller human resources staff than had been present in the past. Management learned that commitment to a well-planned, basic strategy improves both operating expenses and gross revenue.

Competency and the Balanced Scorecard

Robert Kaplan and David Norton have proposed a system of performance measurement that goes beyond the traditional model by building a future orientation.[5] It is called the Balanced Scorecard and it is attracting a lot of attention as well as trials. Their rationale is that the income statement and the balance sheet are indices of what has happened in the past. Given the rate of speed of the marketplace today, the sixteenth-century accounting model on which we have built our performance evaluation systems is too slow and too late. The authors argue that we need leading rather than lagging indicators and that we need to look beyond standard accounting to predictive models.

The Balanced Scorecard displays several categories. Typically, they include technology, customer service, innovation, and new financial perspectives. Some applications of the model place customer and employee factors in a human category. Examples on the customer side would be retention and repeat sales. The employee side might include competency, succession planning, retention, learning, and commitment. Standards in these areas are easy enough to design. Even the psychological factor of commitment can be assessed through employee surveys. Once something like competencies are clearly defined, they can be measured.

It is clear that organizations are coming around to the idea that managing in the new century is going to be even more novel and complex than they had feared. Given a marketplace of ever accelerating high speeds, uncertainty, increasing competitiveness, and new customer needs and expectations, companies have to find and commit themselves to something extremely fundamental on which to build their plans and systems. This is a core strategy.

Quantum Leaps

In *Jumping the Curve,* Nicholas Imparato and Oren Harari state that for many managers today, a tough fact of life is that the world is becoming starkly different from what they knew and counted on.[6] The authors suggest that managers now have three choices. The first is to attempt to hide out until retirement, which is becoming more difficult as companies continue to slim down, exposing the noncontributors. The second is to develop new skills and attitudes and commit themselves to more than survival. The third is to quit.

The authors demand that managers accept their role as shifting from being directors of work to becoming agents of change. I have a slight correction to make. We don't need any more change agents. Typical self-styled agents of change act like the smart aleck who throws a stink bomb into a room and slams the door. When everyone is sufficiently nauseated he comes in and suggests there is a need for some fresh air. What we need instead are *leaders* of change and *guarantors* of customer satisfaction. This means managers as leaders of change must make a commitment to an everlasting strategy to assess every aspect of their function and to reinvent most of it if they are to survive in the twenty-first century.

Commitment to reinvention starts with values, strategy, and culture. Next, it requires leadership and, finally, appropriate processes. Only after that should management worry about investing in technology. Buying a mess of computers is much easier than reinventing the values, strategy, culture, and systems that will produce continuous value for the customer.

The redesigned values, strategy, and culture are the foundation for your future. The first step in making the quantum leap off that base requires projecting the market opportunities five or more years ahead. That new foundation, then, is like the runway of a pole vault. It must provide solid and reliable footing, not be slippery. The vision of the future is the crossbar. It tells you the height you are trying to achieve, and suggests the speed and strength required to reach it. Your operating systems and required competencies are the pole for vaulting over the bar. They provide the leverage.

Strategic Commitment to the Future

According to Hamel and Prahalad, a strategy that focuses on product lines and market share in the current market is doomed. Planning cannot be incremental in today's warp-speed markets. By the time we figure out how to hold our own or gain ground in today's game, someone will have changed the rules. We can bring in the best football coach and players in the world, but when the game changes to soccer we're in trouble. Commitment to strategic planning as it's been done since 1950 is a bad decision. Managers need a new notion of what it means to be strategic. *Strategic* implies a core focus, not a paper plan.

On Florida's east coast just south of the space center, Michael Means is demonstrating what a future-oriented strategy looks like.

Rather than making strategic plans to hold market share for his Holmes Regional Medical Center or positioning it for acquisition by an HMO, he's building a new structure of health care for the region. Means's idea is that survival and excellence in patient care in the twenty-first century will require something fundamentally different from a market populated by independent health care providers each looking out for his/her/their own share. His concept of twenty-first-century health care requires commitment on the part of all providers—from the physicians through the vendors and the medical facilities—to an approach that acknowledges the verities of the twenty-first century rather than the nineteenth. Win or lose, saddling up for the future is more effective than trying to corral the present.

The distinction between current strategic planning and strategic architecturing is described by Gary Hamel and C. K. Prahalad,[7] as seen in Figure 3-2. Many of the themes in strategic architecturing mirror or imply the practices of the BHAMs. We can see connections to strategic commitment, communication, partnering and collaboration, innovation and risk, and competitive passion. Underlying it all is the idea of values, strategy, and culture.

> **BHAM Lesson:** *Long-term success demands sustained commitment to a core strategy.*

From the comparison made in Figure 3-2, we can see the great difference between traditional strategic planning and strategic architecturing. The survey shown in Figure 3-3 contains questions whose answers will show you which path your organization is taking. The higher the level of agreement with the sentences given, the more futuristic is your strategic commitment.

Summary

All available research confirms that long-term success requires long-term commitment to a core strategy. This is the second way in which top management builds an enduring institution. Core strategy is a natural outgrowth of the values and vision of the com-

Figure 3-2. Characteristics of strategic planning vs. strategic architecturing.

	Strategic Planning	*Strategic Architecturing*
Planning Goal	▫ Incremental improvement in market share & position	▫ Rewriting industry rules and creating new competitive space
Planning Process	▫ Formulaic and ritualistic ▫ Existing industry & market structure as the baseline ▫ Industry structure analysis (segmentation, value chain, cost structure, competitor benchmarking, etc.) ▫ Tests for fit between resources and plans ▫ Capital budgeting and allocation of resources among competing projects	▫ Exploratory and open-ended ▫ An understanding of discontinuities and competencies as the baseline ▫ A search for new functionalities or new ways of delivering traditional functionalities ▫ Enlarging opportunity horizons ▫ Tests for significance and timeliness of new opportunities ▫ Development of plans for competence acquisition and migration ▫ Development of opportunity approach plans ▫ The corporation as the unit of analysis
Planning Resources	▫ Business unit executives ▫ Few experts ▫ Staff-driven	▫ Many managers ▫ Collective wisdom of the company ▫ Line-and staff-driven

Source: Gary Hamel and C. K. Prahalad, *Competing for the Future* (Boston: Harvard Business School Press, 1994), p. 283.

Figure 3-3. Futures strategy survey.

1. Management has a clear, collective view of future market possibilities.

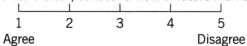

   1   2   3   4   5
   Agree   Disagree

2. Management has developed a system for building core competencies, deploying new functionalities, and serving customers in the twenty-first-century market.

   1   2   3   4   5
   Agree   Disagree

3. Management has communicated its view of the future to all employees.

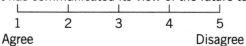

   1   2   3   4   5
   Agree   Disagree

4. Management has built in a significant amount of stretch to inspire employees.

   1   2   3   4   5
   Agree   Disagree

5. Employees agree with and are truly committed to management's vision of the future.

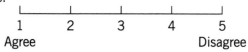

   1   2   3   4   5
   Agree   Disagree

6. Management has started the company on the road to the future with explicit sets of strategic goals and tactical objectives.

   1   2   3   4   5
   Agree   Disagree

7. There is a deep sense of urgency throughout the company regarding the future vision.

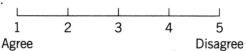

   1   2   3   4   5
   Agree   Disagree

8. There is ample evidence that management is as committed to developing core competencies as it is to other issues.

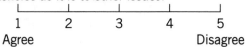

| 1 | 2 | 3 | 4 | 5 |
| Agree | | | | Disagree |

9. We are testing management's vision with a sufficient number of trials in the market to ensure that we are on the leading edge of the learning curve.

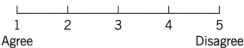

| 1 | 2 | 3 | 4 | 5 |
| Agree | | | | Disagree |

10. The launching of the future vision has created a great deal of excitement around the company.

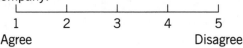

| 1 | 2 | 3 | 4 | 5 |
| Agree | | | | Disagree |

Source: Adapted from Gary Hamel and C. K. Prahalad, *Competing for the Future* (Boston: Harvard Business School Press, 1994), pp. 294–296.

pany. Values and strategic commitment combined form two of the three structural foundations of the organization. Culture is the third.

The missing element in most strategic planning is the human being. Plans and resources are inert. People are the exception. They are the catalyst. It's easier to ignore them and focus on the sterile planning exercise. However, all organizational elements, including plans, don't do anything but gather dust until people pull them off the shelf and launch them. The latest form of corporate performance measurement, the Balanced Scorecard, acknowledges that human competence, learning, and commitment are leading indicators of performance. The future needs commitment to leading rather than lagging indices of performance.

Future markets will belong to those who set aside standard strategic planning for a core commitment to future architecturing. Executives in the BHAM companies are looking not at how to sustain market share in this marketplace but rather at how to redesign the emerging market to suit their competencies and functionalities.

Those who can handle current problems while keeping their eyes on the future will be the winners in the next millennium.

References

1. Michael Treacy and Fred Wiersema, *The Discipline of Market Leaders* (Reading, Mass.: Addison-Wesley, 1995).
2. Ibid., p. xv.
3. David McClellan, *A Guide to Job Competence Assessment* (Boston: McBer, 1976).
4. Lyle Spencer and Signe Spencer, *Competence at Work* (New York: John Wiley & Sons, 1993), pp. 9–11.
5. Robert Kaplan and David Norton, "The Balanced Scorecard, Measures That Drive Performance," *Harvard Business Review*, January–February 1992, pp. 71–79.
6. Nicholas Imparato and Oren Harari, *Jumping the Curve* (San Francisco: Jossey-Bass, 1994), p. 56.
7. Gary Hamel and C. K. Prahalad, *Competing for the Future* (Boston: Harvard Business School Press, 1994), p. 283.

4

Culture-System Linkage

How the Best Use Corporate Culture in Policy, System, and Process Design to Reinforce Values and Stimulate High Performance

> Culture: *"the sum total of ways of living built up by a group of human beings, which is transmitted from one generation to another."*
>
> —American Collegiate Dictionary

Organizational culture is a paradox itself. In one way it is everywhere; in another, it is invisible. Culture is a concept created by and for the human elements of a community. In business organizations it starts with the corporate belief system. This is composed of beliefs, attitudes, and values. These are the less visible elements, which are the most enduring. Key members of management may leave, and the business may even shift primary product lines; still the belief system persists. Part of the reason why the basic values are hard to change is that people don't think about them. They have been accepted and internalized long ago.

From these most basic elements come the more visible behavioral norms. These might be called the *style* of the company. We don't have to be in an organization very long before we catch on to the norms. It starts when we walk through the door and see how people are dressed and what the work space looks like. When we are greeted, interviewed, or taken on a tour, we see and feel the culture through the words, gestures, and interactions of the people we encounter along the way. It isn't easy to change these manifestations of a culture either, but it's less difficult than trying to change the corporate values.

Terry Deal and Allan Kennedy brought this topic to management's attention with their popular work *Corporate Cultures*.[1] They studied eighty companies in search of variables that "make for consistently outstanding company performance." Through a reductive analysis they identified eighteen organizations that had clearly communicated qualitative beliefs. Every one of the eighteen was an outstanding performer. They went on to conclude that strong cultures are powerful levers for guiding employee behavior in two ways:

> *"A strong culture is a system of informal rules that spells out how people are to behave most of the time. A strong culture helps people feel better about what they do, so they are more likely to work harder."*

Conscious Use of Culture

The difference between the BHAMs and The Rest is that the BHAMs don't treat culture as a passive condition. In our most recent follow-up research with the BHAMs, we have found that managers are focusing on culture even more than they did in the past. They are aware of how it affects everything and they are increasing their efforts to bring its power into their plans and programs. Many CEOs understand that one of their major responsibilities is in fact to create and manage culture.

Historically, founders of America's most successful corporations knew that they had to create an environment in which employees could feel they were part of a "family." In this corporate womb they could be secure and successful. Messrs. Procter and Gamble at P&G, Watson at IBM, Hewlett and Packard at H-P, Mary Kay at Mary Kay Cosmetics, and other founding fathers and mothers consciously exhibited culture as an active force.

Research by Saratoga Institute and others over the past decade has shown the power of culture on everything from motivation to retention and productivity. The BHAMs understand that if they align their strategy and systems with their culture, they will obtain numerous benefits.

First, a cohesive culture does not guarantee long-term superior performance, but it clearly has an effect on it. In companies with strong cultures, the organization is better able to weather rapid growth and serious declines in business volume and profitability. Where people buy into the company because they like living in its culture, they are supportive in tough times and make the extra effort when business volume outstrips resources.

Second, cultures take a long time to change—for better or for worse. But when the people move as a group with a shifting culture, stress is reduced. There is a "misery loves company" type of atmosphere, wherein everyone pitches in because they identify with each other, with management, and with the goals of the organization.

Third, the culture acts as a self-policing force. Everyone knows what is acceptable, what is expected, and what is taboo. As a result, management seldom has to take drastic action to whip a deviant into line. Peers do it for them.

Fourth, culture can turn negative. If and when management acts without sensitivity or with downright orneryness for an extended period, people begin to respond in kind. A culture that was very positive and cooperative can become contentious, selfish, or even destructive. At the least, people withhold their commitment to the company. They may begin to band together in opposition to management by inviting in a union, or engage in even more drastic actions such as sabotage. When this becomes a companywide practice, the negative culture dooms any attempt at improving performance.

As the human component becomes the critical variable of the Information Age, factors such as culture take on more importance. Culture is people, not cash, equipment, facilities, or even a superior product. In a service business, one might say without too much reservation that culture is the critical variable. A positive culture envelops customers. It can make up for lack of resources or even mediocre product. Take a bank, restaurant, or retail store, for example. If a culture becomes negative, no amount of money can turn or enlist the imagination and energy of the workforce. Incentive pay may release the pressure for a time, but in the end it creates a band of mercenaries. Employees in dysfunctional cultures ignore customers. Sometimes they "hide," making it difficult for the customer to buy. Employees don't offer help or suggestions—or sell up. On the other hand, charismatic leaders can turn a culture positive by selling a new vision. Sam Walton's contribution beyond his inventory systems was the vision he sold his employees and the excitement he created. He made the sale, and his people built a strongly positive culture that welcomed shoppers. Once management loses its employees' hearts and spirits, the culture takes on a plague-like atmosphere, affecting everyone who comes in contact with it. If this develops, it may take years to win back the trust of the workforce. A more effective strategy is to build a positive culture from the beginning.

A word of caution is due here. There is a correlation between a strong culture and financial performance. However, the correlation is moderate. Culture is not the only factor in driving performance. Companies still need a clear vision, a commitment to a strategy that makes sense, and the systems and resources necessary to carry out the vision and strategy.

Culture as Social Architecture

One way of viewing culture is as the social architecture of the organization. It is that belief system around which behavior is constructed. I prefer to think of culture as an edifice, as the foundation of human interaction. It is the wall that defines the boundaries and the roof that covers and protects the inhabitants from outside elements.

It is in the same enclosure that culture can become a barrier to progress. Social structure intensifies certain views and biases. At the same time, it excludes or overwhelms others. One danger is that people may forget why they believe what they believe. It's like the story of the woman who always cut the end off a roast before putting it in the oven. When her husband asked why she did this, she replied that her mother had always done it. The husband then asked his mother-in-law why she did it, and she stated: "I had a smaller roasting pan and oven than you do." The second danger is that over time people will turn inward and come to believe that what they don't know isn't worth knowing. The mores of the culture become eternal truths that are not to be questioned. This kind of reverence for the past then becomes an insurmountable barrier to progress.

Values, Strategy, Culture

Collectively, values, strategy, and culture are the foundation on which not only behavior but business plans are erected. These three are the antecedents of the organizational systems. Collectively, they drive everything in the organization. Specifically, culture drives systems design, which in turn influences human behavior. Behavior leads to job performance and, ultimately, to results (as seen in Figure 4-1).

Most of the time, management constructs new programs or systems/processes on the value-strategy-culture base without thinking much about it. But once in a while someone introduces a new program that conflicts with that base. If it is a new benefit, as performance review process or other program that directly affects people rather than, say, a manufacturing process, it may clash with the culture.

For example, let's assume you have a company with a fairly freewheeling culture. It's not exactly a laissez-faire style, but innovation and risk taking are encouraged. Egalitarianism is definitely your model of operation. You don't have a lot of structure and rules, but you do have value accountability and you do celebrate individual heroics. Into this atmosphere a new chief executive introduces the performance management system used in his old company, STOLID, INC. The new system is very formal. It requires each supervisor to set objectives and give them to his subordinates. After all, the CEO reckons, you hire supervisors to supervise. If

Figure 4-1. The culture-performance chain.

CULTURE SYSTEMS → BEHAVIOR → PERFORMANCE

they don't know what their people should be doing and achieving, you need to get new supervisors. The forms are lengthy and totally focused on objectives. Either you make the objective or you don't. There is some discussion in the process, but not a lot of room for change. Formal reviews are to be strictly adhered to.

How well do you think this new method is going to be received? The rules of engagement have been summarily changed. The old style of open discourse has been thrown over for rigid forms and one-way communications. One of two things will happen. If the new CEO persists in pushing this approach, the culture will change gradually and some people will begin to look elsewhere for employment. Maybe that's the new guy's real agenda. The other possibility is that your culture is too strong. It might subvert or overwhelm the new process, which in time will die, and the new guy will be gone. Either way, the new system is a disruptive idea.

Corporate culture is like a deep, fast-flowing river. If you want to change its direction, it is easier to cut a new channel and let it gradually seek the new level than it is to try damming up its force.

Two Cultures, Two Systems

BHAMs understand how important a strong culture can be. They also understand how to use it interactively with systems to support their style and to drive the organization in the direction they want it to go. A case in point is provided by the different methods that two companies with different cultures used in similar situations.

One is a fast-growing, highly successful financial services company. It has nearly 4,000 employees and is headquartered in the Southeast. The culture is what might be described as "wide open." It is highly intense, fast-paced, very ambitious, egalitarian, and involving. When this company designed its employee recognition program, it matched the culture. Employees party hard when it comes time to celebrate something. Exceptional performance is recognized in front of the whole group with great fanfare. They throw a minicarnival.

The second is a manufacturing company. It makes automated industrial machinery and precision instruments for the aerospace industry. There is a strong engineering ethic in place. This company, located in the Northeast, has about 3,000 employees. The culture here is driven by the need for exactitude since half the company's business is with Uncle Sam's space program. Management has fought off the tendency to be bureaucratic by focusing on trust in individuals and empowerment for all. The atmosphere is professional and respectful. When someone performs beyond requirements and recognition is due, there is little fanfare. No banners, theatrics, or gimmicks are employed. The high performer is simply given his reward with truly personal and heartfelt thanks.

Now, imagine what it would be like in this low-key environment if they put together some circus-type celebration. The recipient would probably go catatonic. Likewise, if you attempted a quiet professional approach in the "wide-open" company, nobody would hear you.

Building Achieving Cultures

Exceptionally effective companies typically exhibit cultlike cultures. Strong cultures, while they do not ensure exceptional performance, do enhance a company's ability to tackle the big challenges successfully. The reason behind this is that the people feel that they are part of something special, members of a group that can accomplish the impossible.

On rare occasions, you may find yourself in a start-up situation where no culture exists beyond the values of the first few adventurers. In this case, you can design the culture you want.

UCS

When AT&T launched its Universal Card Services business in the late 1980s, it purposely started it a long way from other AT&T facilities. Management wanted the initial group to establish a new kind of culture that emphasized entrepreneurial traits.

The top management group at UCS was determined to provide quality products that consistently exceeded customer expectations while simultaneously making the company a fun place in which to work. This culture was built on three elements:

1. *Customer delight.* They don't try to satisfy customers, they delight them.
2. *Associate delight.* Employees are regarded as crucial to the business's success and are referred to as "associates." Management's job is to delight the associates.
3. *Continuous improvement.* Never being satisfied is UCS's basic premise.

Innovation and risk taking are at the heart of the UCS culture. Management encourages associates to accept challenges and take risks. In order to show they really mean it, Fred Winkler, executive vice president of customer service, created the Power of One award to recognize associates who act on their own to delight a customer. As part of the fun aspect of the culture, celebrations are the norm when someone is rewarded. Everyone makes a big deal out of recognizing the performance.

The UCS philosophy is that if the company delights its associates, the associates will carry that feeling over to customer relations. This belief is corroborated by the work of Leonard Schlesinger and James Heskett.[2] Their research demonstrated that employee attitudes carry over into their interactions with customers. This makes sense. Happy, motivated employees go the extra mile for customers. Customers return and refer the company to their friends. One case of good service usually yields at least three referrals. Bad service generates negative remarks to as many as ten potential customers.

UCS management knows that it is important to respond quickly to the opinions of associates. An example of how associates are rewarded for their extra efforts is the ten-minute massage. One UCS associate suggested that since many people work at their computers eight hours a day, the company should hire a masseuse to deal with backaches, muscle cramps, and fatigue. After some consideration, the company agreed, and now the masseuse is available for the ten-minute special every Tuesday and Thursday.

Associates are also given the opportunity to learn about other jobs. Under the Associate of the Day program anyone can sign up to observe what others do in their jobs. Subject-matter experts give half-hour presentations, or associates may shadow managers for a day. This accomplishes two things. First, if people want to pursue other fields, they can get a realistic look at the work being done. Second, workers in one area can see what is done in other areas. This helps them in making decisions that will affect others. The by-product of seeing what is happening on the other side of the fence is increased understanding, cross-functional efficiency, and cohesiveness. It is clear to everyone at UCS that *we* are in this together.

The list of things that are done to instill and reinforce the culture of self-reliance as well as that of togetherness seems endless. Management wanted to build a working environment that championed certain behaviors. So, they put their brains and money where their mouth was and created a culture that would support the values and strategy of the new company. From the beginning, UCS communicated the strategies it was operating on to all associates. Everyone was trusted to know where the company intended to go. All activities were then directed toward those strategies. Recognition of the application of corporate values and strategies is swift, positive, and powerful. And despite the exceptional results that UCS achieved in its first five years, there is no sense of complacency here. In this company, the only direction to go is up.

Despite the great early success of UCS, as this goes to press, the company has been struggling. The credit card market is changing. Economic forces, spending, and paying habits of credit card users are changing. It remains to be seen what the company can do to respond. Also of interest will be the effect it has on the culture. If management abandons the sense of innovation and excitement that led to its early success in favor of a tightening-down and loss of faith in the employees, the company could be severely damaged. It is easy to be enthusiastic in good times. Management must keep faith with the people and trust in them to carry out a new strategy that will be responsive to the changing marketplace. Otherwise, it will be another case study of failure to move with the times.

Managing Networks

The cultural network is a powerful underground communications conduit.[3] At one level is the content of corporate communications. This includes the words that are used in memos, e-mail bulletins, newsletters, and announcements of any kind. At another, underground level is the meaning of the communiqués. Here is where people go when they want to know what all these things really mean. The communicators can be anyone whom people will listen to. Even mail room employees can be important interpreters if they keep their eyes and ears open. They're at the hub of most written communications. If they're astute, they learn to read between the lines. Just the look on the face of someone who gives them a bulletin to distribute can be a tip-off that this is serious—or nonsense. What really matters in an organization is the underground network's interpretation of an event, not the formal event itself.

Since perception is reality to the perceiver, managers must be sensitive to the way in which they do things. As my wife has told me many times, "Honey, it's not so much what you do as the way you do it that makes a difference." Process is sometimes more important than content.

Tapping into the network is a relatively easy task. There are six definable steps.

1. Cultivate your own network by finding and making contact with the translators. Start by asking who might know about a certain issue or event.
2. Treat everyone with the respect due a translator, because anyone might be one, regardless of his or her position in the hierarchy.
3. Act ignorant and ask people to tell you what something means or to recount some historical anecdote. It makes them feel important, and their replies tell you if they are translators.
4. Ask for referrals to others who may be able to tell you what is happening. People in the network, if they trust you, will pass you on to others in the network.
5. Encourage the storytellers to translate. That is their role and they want and expect to play it.
6. Use the network to carry the hidden message that can't be spoken. If your relationship with a translator is solid, you won't have to spell out the details. He or she will pick up your meaning and move it along the network.

BHAMs seem to be very adept at managing their networks. It's probably because they see beyond the obvious and visible.

They know how important culture and communications are for moving their people.

It could be that the people who lead BHAM companies are very sensitive to the impact of the soft side of management (i.e., human relations). If you intend to move people consistently without resorting to bribery or force, you have to deal with them from their point of view. By talking openly, honestly, and consistently with them, involving them in decisions and actions, listening to their ideas, and, more importantly, responding to them, you show that you respect them. That does more to build loyalty and commitment than any incentive pay program.

Coping With and Co-Opting Subcultures

Despite our strong emphasis on the power of the corporate culture, we have to recognize the legitimacy of subcultures. Every organization has subcultures, which often form around functional or geographic divisions. Clearly, a corporate division in Maine is unlikely to share many cultural traits with a division in New Mexico. The visible elements of these traits include ways of dressing, ways of speaking, work habits, and physical settings. These bonding factors are important because they tell everyone whether or not an employee is *one of us*. If you transfer people from the plant in Albuquerque to the service center in Freeport, the new arrivals are generally greeted with some degree of aloofness until they prove, by adopting the local customs, their desire to join the subculture.

For top management, the paradox lies in trying to keep one corporate culture as the overriding uniting force while simultaneously allowing subcultures to flourish. There is no point in trying to suppress subcultures. They just go deeper underground and become even less trusting of others outside their group. This is where the strong, superordinate cultures of the BHAMs prove themselves. BHAMs have shown us that it is more effective to openly accept and appreciate the subculture and then to put forth the virtues of the corporate culture as a megacultural rallying point.

Crossing Borders

We have heard stories about dealing with foreign cultures. The differences between Maine and New Mexico are nothing compared to the gulf between France and Germany or the United States and Japan or even Mexico and Venezuela. Personally, I find coping with international cultures a fascinating but sometimes tiring exercise. You never know when you're about to put your foot in your mouth. I find it best to stay back a bit and watch before assuming that the foreign associate shares my frame of mind.

Effective culture managers are trained in how to understand and account for different perceptions of management's role, different performance expectations and rewards, different hierarchical norms, and different societal rituals. For example, if you are doing business in a Muslim country, you should allow extra time at lunch for people to go to the mosque and pray. Learn that in some places friendship is the basis for business, not the other way around. Don't expect Venezuelans at an oil refinery on a peninsula north of Maracaibo to be as punctual as Swiss bankers will be at a meeting in Zurich. I'll cover the cross-culture issue later, in Chapter 9, as a continuous improvement factor. Finally, as a wise man once advised me, "When eating for the first time in a foreign country, make believe that the unknown entrée is chicken and just eat it!" And it's best not to ask later what it was even if you liked it!

Changing Cultures

Over the past ten years much has been made of the need to change corporate cultures. It is true that some of the most successful cultures failed to advance in keeping with the demands of the new world market. A deeply entrenched culture makes implementing radically new strategies very difficult. The best-known example of this is IBM. This company once owned 60 percent of the computer market. For twenty years it was a global powerhouse of unparalleled dimensions. If in 1985 anyone had suggested that IBM had peaked and was in for a major overhaul, that person would have been laughed out of the room. Only five years later, we saw just that happen. As the computing market focus shifted from mainframes to mini- and microcomputers, then to software, and on to networking, the market transformed from hardware manufacturing to information management. But IBM's cultural mind-set was locked so tightly that a new paradigm could not penetrate it.

The company is a classic example of Gordon Donaldson and Jay Lorsch's discovery.[4] From a study of a dozen large U.S. companies, they found the following consistent pattern:

1. Strong founders establish corporate cultures that are internally consistent and sensible in the light of prevailing conditions.
2. These cultures facilitate managerial decision making.
3. If the environment doesn't change radically, a company can be successful for decades with only minor modifications of the culture.
4. If, on the other hand, an industry changes significantly, culture change is often too slow to prevent serious deterioration in financial performance.

The turnaround of a culture as embedded as IBM's was wrenching, to say the least. More often than not, an outsider is brought in as CEO to be the catalyst for change that was missing within. Today, IBM has an outside CEO for the first time in history. Tens of thousands of employees have been let go in one way or another. Restructuring is the company's major preoccupation in the 1990s. And the blue-suit, white-shirt culture that made so much sense in the 1950s and 1960s is a thing of the past at IBM. With structural and cultural changes in place, a foundation has been laid for a new look at the information market. The two questions for every top executive team, and this includes the board of directors, are: "How do we avoid growing a culture that strangles the company?" and "How do we use systems to change the culture?"

The Power of the CEO

As with everything else, the CEO drives the culture. The evidence is clear that the single most powerful factor behind successful culture change is competent leadership at the top of the organization. Intuitively, people look to the boss for strategic leadership. When a clear vision isn't forthcoming, they often become confused and disheartened. They flounder and waste time looking for signals. The famous culture change cases of the past twenty years were all driven by and carried through on the strength of leadership shown by the chairman or president. Close examination of the cases suggests that there are two other factors common to successful change. They are an outsider's perspective and an inside power base.

An outsider seems necessary in the most critical cases because he can bring a fresh, more venturesome perspective and less emotional attachment to the existing culture. Obviously, the typical insider is thoroughly indoctrinated in the culture and therefore less able to question it or to see the need for momentous change. Roger Smith at General Motors and John Akers at IBM are examples. Nearly all the executives who have led successful changes have come from outside the firm or at least from outside the "core" businesses. Jack Welch of General Electric is an example of an inside-outsider in that he came up through the plastics business of GE, a sector that is not one of the mainstream business lines of the corporation.

One of the most famous recent cases is that of Apple Computer. Through several major changes of the top executive group the company continued to lose market share. From a point it once occupied as a celebrated icon of the computing world, it steadily dropped to less than a 7 percent market share by early 1996. Finally, the board ousted both founder Mike Markkula and his hand-picked president, Michael Spindler, in favor of an outsider.

The third hallmark, an inside power base, can be seen as necessary when the implementation of a change strategy is being considered. The first thing the effective leaders did was to create an atmosphere of urgency, if not one of crisis. They created measurement systems outside the traditional financial reports to obtain the data they needed to demonstrate the validity of their claims. They communicated a clear, compelling vision of the changes required. These were communicated by both word and deed. Here is the telling point: They spent much more time talking and listening to their employees than had their predecessors.

They built their power base in one of two ways. Some brought in a number of top executives to help drive the change. Others appealed to the values of the old management group to bring them on board the change vehicle. They helped everyone see what was truly a core value versus what was an artifact of the culture that could be dispensed with without selling out their values. Operating objectives, strategies, and practices were differentiated from core values. People began to see that they could change the company while hanging onto some of their basic values. Finally, to give credibility to the new vision, the CEOs looked for some quick hits. They needed a few early positive results to recognize those who had supported the change strategy and to strengthen people for the long haul.

In every case the change took years rather than months. On average, it took more than six years. In a couple of cases it has been going on for ten years, with continual modification. It takes a long time to develop the motivation to be part of the change. But once it is there its power can be employed to carry the many process changes required.

The Customer's Impact on Culture Change

In the final analysis, all strategies and culture changes must be driven by a view of market trends and changing customer requirements. Hamel and Prahalad offer the first steps on the path to finding the appropriate strategy.[5] They suggest that you look five to ten years into the future and answer these questions:

1. Which customers will you be serving?
2. Through what channels will you reach customers?
3. Who will be your competitors?
4. What will be the basis for your competitive advantage?
5. Where will your margins come from?
6. What skills or capabilities will make you unique?
7. In what end-product markets will you participate?

While you are contemplating these strategic issues, I suggest that you turn simultaneously to your culture and values. Ask yourself these three questions:

1. What kind of company do you want yours to be in the future?
2. How should it fit in your industry and in your community?
3. What kind of place will your company be to work in then?

Collectively, the answers will raise cultural considerations. Rather than waiting for the strategy to drive the culture, you would do better to look simultaneously at all three structural stones. See Figure 4-2 as an example.

You may find that it is somewhat difficult to answer the value and culture parts. It's not uncommon for an executive team to focus primarily on strategy and then back into values and ignore or downplay culture. This is because it assumes that the culture is more passive than active. The hard, undeniable truth is that culture whispers in the ear of all telling them *how* to play out any new strategy. The way culture and strategy work together can be seen in this simple example: Assume your culture is highly consensual and you see your company moving into a market with extremely short lead times and tiny windows of opportunity. Doesn't this suggest that you need to gear up the speed of the culture? Consensus may have to be modified by a call to action. After all, reaching agreement on a dead issue is a fruitless activity.

Industry Change and Culture

Health care is a perfect example of how outside factors have forced change on internal cultures. The health care business in the United

Figure 4-2. Future view of operations, values, strategy, and culture.

Operational Factor	Values	Implications for Strategy	Culture
1. Customers			
2. Channels			
3. Competitors			
4. Advantage			
5. Margins			
6. Capabilities			
7. Markets			

States is undergoing one of the most massive transformations of any industry in our history. In case after case over the past ten years, we have seen almost total changes in the cultures of many medical institutions.

Through the 1970s, hospitals were known for having rigid rules and hierarchies with no concern for costs and for paying little attention to the feelings of patients and their families. The culture was dominated by the physicians; others in the pecking order received little respect. Patients were treated like cattle in Admitting and their families were shunted aside to a waiting room. Information was passed around sparingly as though it were the combination to the safe. The only positive thing that could be said for many facilities was that the medical staff was dedicated to curing the sick and mending the broken. As human institutions, they left a lot of room for improvement.

In the late 1980s, as the full effects of the government's diagnostically related group (DRG) reimbursements were being felt on service income, the wiser, less ossified institutions and individuals began to change. Accelerating the change was technological advancement, which allowed caregivers to handle more cases on an outpatient basis. The combination of these two forces drove medical center managers to reinvent their business.

VALLEY CHILDREN'S HOSPITAL

Valley Children's Hospital is a model of the new health care culture. VCH is a pediatric facility in Fresno, California, servicing a 65,000-square-mile area in California's Central Valley. It is the only rural pediatric care center in the country. VCH's vision is to provide patients and their families with quality care and exceptional service. VCH also cares about all its employees, recognizing each one's uniqueness and personal need to contribute. The culture supports innovation through mutual respect and a stated desire to have fun doing it. Senior staff members are willing to try new strategies. They empower their people to look for better ways to accomplish tasks, thus meeting the needs of the patients, the employees, and the hospital.

Recognizing how important it is for management to live the culture by example, the hospital puts newly hired managers through an orientation course that includes meetings with all the senior staff and the department heads. This gives them the full treatment on the culture of VCH. After they start working, all managers are evaluated by a new performance management system on two criteria: (1) how they meet corporate expectations on nine topics, and (2) the achievement of strategic goals.

The nine topics on the manager performance checklist are:

1. Culture and mission support
2. Fiscal responsibility
3. Leadership/management style
4. Quality assurance and client satisfaction
5. Human resources development
6. Planning and analysis
7. Communications
8. Personal and professional growth
9. Unit-specific factors

These topics were chosen by the executive committee as critical for business and organizational success. Managers must meet the performance criteria on all nine in order to be eligible for a salary increase.

Goal accomplishment is the second phase of the managerial performance system. Here the strategic operating objectives are set and monitored. A leadership advisory committee meets monthly to help the executive committee set goals and review results. Supervisors and managers are encouraged to sit in since they are the *owners* of the subsequent goals. Achievement of the goals and objectives is also required for a salary increase. Lest you think all this is an overly burdensome challenge, keep in mind that every manager has personal contact with every senior executive. Managers are invited to call on the executives as needed. VCH's dual emphasis on human and financial matters is a living example of the balanced value fixation described in Chapter 2.

Employees also have strong roles to play. A two-way communications system was designed to foster employee involvement and trust. Periodic surveys are conducted with all employees. These are followed by focus groups. Many companies do that. VCH's system is different in that it responds directly to the people with the findings. A response document listing the resulting plans and actions is distributed to all employees. Comment cards on internal cooperation and service are used to evaluate internal customer satisfaction across units.

No system runs error-free. From time to time someone gets upset. A system was developed to deal effectively and fairly with complaints. It starts when a complaint or a formal grievance is filed. Grievances are handled through an equity appeal process that obviates the traditional confrontations of an arbitration meeting. Under this procedure grievances can be resolved at any of several levels:

❑ Through a director
❑ Through a dual review process that includes peer review
❑ Through the chief operating officer

Most grievances are resolved through the dual review process. Usually the peer review committee of five employees makes a recommendation and it is accepted by the vice president involved. The grievance system has helped the hospital avoid costly litigation, improve employee relations, and decrease turnover. Through the peer review committee, employees with grievances feel they have a fair hearing.

VCH's culture is notable for open communication, mutual respect, and personal involvement at all levels. These mores were consciously developed and systematically supported in answer to a changing marketplace. They are reinforced throughout the hospital's operating and administrative systems. A large part of the success of VCH's culture change has come from the directional power of the new systems. As a result of the application of these linked culture/system drivers, the hospital has been able to change a high-pressure, high-risk environment into a place where people like to come to work and where patients are thankful for the supportive atmosphere. On the business side, it has helped VCH achieve an enviably low level of turnover.

Checklist for Culture Building

Strong cultures are not an accidental result. Management puts a great deal of thought and effort into designing, implementing, and sustaining a specific culture. Examples of the lengths to which companies go to establish and reinforce a desired culture are shown in Figure 4-3. No one company does all these things. But

Figure 4-3. Culture-building activities designed by management.

- ❑ Top management continually preaches and models the corporate ideology.
- ❑ Extensive applicant screening processes place a premium on personal fit with the culture.
- ❑ New hire orientation and training programs build in cultural content and are delivered in a manner that reflects the company's values, norms, and traditions.
- ❑ Hiring mostly at the entry level and promoting from within link corporate and employee values from the beginning.
- ❑ Changing the common label of employee to associate or cast member gives formal clues to relationships and expectations.
- ❑ Egalitarian beliefs played out through on-the-job social activities involving all levels proclaim a "work together, play together" ethic.
- ❑ Frequent referral to corporate legends and the company's mythology bonds people to the culture by making them part of something exciting.
- ❑ Development of a corporate jargon, special words, and acronyms creates an internal language that only *one of us* understands.
- ❑ Recreational and informal games, contests, incentives, and public recognition celebrate successes consistent with the corporate ideal.
- ❑ Office layout and furniture are deliberately chosen to provide visible reinforcement of the norms and the rewards for playing the game.
- ❑ Internal training systems function as surrogate universities, controlling training content and generating alumni feelings.
- ❑ Performance objectives and advancement standards are linked with the corporate philosophy.
- ❑ Rewards and penalties are abundant for those who exemplify or flaunt the corporate dogma.
- ❑ Employees are encouraged to commit themselves to the values through extra effort and/or financial investment.

you probably recognize some of them: Motorola's university, Disney's use of "cast member" in place of the traditional "employee" designator, Wal-Mart's songs and cheerleading at meetings, Hewlett-Packard's stories of Bill and Dave starting the business in their garage, Apple and Tandem's Friday afternoon beer busts for employees, General Electric's Crotonville management center, Federal Express's Fred Smith recounting getting a C on his master's thesis, which laid out the plan for a new package delivery industry.

Cultures develop with or without help. The BHAMs understand that molding a strong culture that can be aligned with their strategy and support their vision gives them a solid structural foundation. Systems are a key tool in cultural management. Culture provides a source of cohesion and strength that helps the company persevere during bad times and make the most of opportunities in good times.

> **BHAM Lesson:** *Culture is a powerful force, which, when linked with systems, drives performance-enhancing behavior.*

Summary

Culture, along with corporate values and commitment to a long-term strategy, is the basis of the organization. Culture is composed of the belief system of the company and the behavioral norms that spring from it. A strong corporate culture can positively affect financial performance. It accomplishes this, first, by aligning and linking people through the values in the belief system. Second, it gives them a common vision that bonds the group and sends it off together in pursuit of the vision and goals. Third, it provides a structure and form of control that make bureaucratic policies unnecessary.

Culture has a power that can be used consciously by linking it with operating and administrative systems. Policies, systems, and processes function most effectively and with the least effort when they are compatible with the culture. Launching a policy or procedure that conflicts with cultural values or norms is a prescription for disaster. Culture can be changed, albeit slowly, through systems. By designing and installing one system after another that espouse new ideals, the culture can be gradually moved in a new direction.

Finally, culture must never become static, rigid, or obsolescent. When it does, the business suffers. Ossification of the culture leads to the not-invented-here syndrome, which is the first step on the road to ruin. This syndrome is particularly evident when the founder is still in charge. It is very difficult psychologically for daddy or mommy to see their baby grow into something they never envisioned. Letting go is the most difficult act in parenthood.

The CEO has the key role in culture change. Effective leadership is a must. Most often, successful change also requires an outsider's perspective. In almost every case, the new CEO must bring the vision of the need to change. Then, a case for urgency must be built by citing changing market and customer demands, as well as the consequences of not meeting those demands. Then, the key is to build power behind the change through systems that empower and stimulate people. The CEO may start by bringing in some key outside executives, but even then the need for change must be sold to current managers who will drive the implementation of the new systems.

A strong culture is not a guarantor of perpetual success. But so long as it moves with the times, it can be a powerful driver of financial performance.

References

1. Terry Deal and Allan A. Kennedy, *Corporate Cultures* (Reading, Mass.: Addison-Wesley, 1982), pp. 7–16.
2. Leonard Schlesinger and James Heskett, "The Service Driven Service Company," *Harvard Business Review*, September–October 1991, pp. 71–81.
3. Deal and Kennedy, p. 86.
4. Gordon Donaldson and Jay Lorsch, *Decision Making at the Top* (New York: Basic Books, 1983).
5. Gary Hamel and C. K. Prahalad, *Competing for the Future* (Boston: Harvard Business School Press, 1994), pp. 16–17.

5

Massive Multidirectional Communications

How the Best's Obsession With 360-Degree Communication and Information Sharing Builds Trust

The two most valuable resources any company has do not appear on its balance sheet. They are information and people. The principal purpose of the balance sheet is to tell your bank how much it can sell your company for if you default on your loan. Perhaps the reason the most valuable assets do not appear here is that the accounting profession isn't able to put a dollar value on people or data. The attempt that was made at human resources accounting in the late 1970s died quickly because the financial community couldn't figure out if people should be appreciated or depreciated over time. In the case of data, maybe they don't appear on the balance sheet because so little is converted into usable information.

Nevertheless, the importance of people and information is finally being acknowledged in what is labeled *intellectual capital.* Someone described intellectual capital as the intelligence that's left behind when people go home at night. This is only partly true. What's left behind is databases, research and development in progress, patents, and other intellectual property. What goes out the door with the people is even more truly intellectual capital. It is the knowledge, skill, experience, and insights that are called "tacit knowledge." This chapter is not a dissertation on intellectual capital because businesspeople won't get excited about it until it hits the balance sheet. Suffice it to say that the interaction of people and information, and the subsequent application of this intellectual capital, is one of the prime distinguishing features of effective organizations.

Communications, or information processing and transmittal, is the most pervasive human activity. It starts with talking to ourselves in response to sensually perceived incoming data and goes all the way to large-scale corporate communications programs. Life is largely taken up with information processing, transmission, and reaction to the information received. The BHAMs utilize the power of multilateral communications. When we talk about communications, we include two-way transmissions. It is obvious that people in organizations need relevant, objective data to make good decisions. Then, after making the decision and taking appropriate action, they send data out and receive data back with which to evaluate their decisions. Management converts data from the economic and regulatory environment, the competition, its customers, and daily operations into information. How, when, why, and to whom it passes on this information determines much of the success of an organization. Figure 5-1 is an illustration of the communication value chain.

The Value of Communications

The value of communication management can be seen in detail by starting before there are any data. Communication's value begins with the wisdom to select and gather useful data—that is, data that are relevant to the organization's current position and future aspirations. This first step is absolutely critical because it is the basis of the GIGO acronym (garbage in-garbage out). Once a database strategy is established—and a database should be a strategy, not a static batch of 1s and 0s—then it has to be selectively tapped to provide input for planning and operations.

This tapping is shown in Figure 5-1 as a combination of skills. They include cognitive and technical skills. Cognitive skills help us view the environment and decide which data are needed. Techni-

Figure 5-1. Communication value chain.

STRATEGY: Who needs to know what to do what?
MANAGEMENT BELIEF SYSTEM: Beliefs, attitudes, and values about organizational communications
TRANSMISSION: Media and communicators
RECEPTION: Audience knowledge and trust

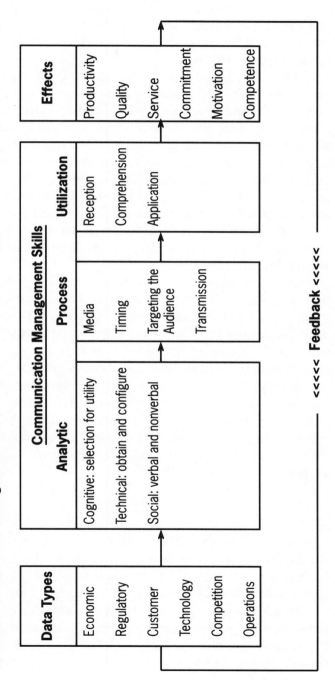

cal skills let us reach into the database and extract what we need in an efficient manner. Increasingly, databases are electronic, but there are still manual extraction methods called reading and periodical clipping services.

After the data are in hand, so to speak, social skills are required for human communications. These include both verbal and nonverbal communications and both individual and group communications. Nonverbal communications are at least as important as verbal communications because often the show is more influential than the words. Consider rock concert light shows, political conventions, and the famous Nuremberg extravaganzas that Albert Speer staged for Hitler in the 1930s. A less intense but more common example is the case of a boss who called a department meeting and said, "We've got to learn to work together," while slamming his fist into the palm of his hand. What do you think he was communicating?

Deciding *which* data to transmit and *how* to transmit the data that have been configured into information are a function of the manager's or the corporation's belief system. Based on the beliefs, attitudes, and values that the transmitter (management) has regarding the receivers (employees or customers), it will select the information to be transmitted and choose the target audience.

Receipt of the transmission generates a certain amount of knowledge and a certain level of trust. This depends on the clarity of the transmission and the type and amount of information transmitted. Employees who are knowledgeable about relevant issues and who believe that they are trusted by management then feel empowered. The formula is:

$$K \times M \times S \times C = V$$

Knowledge times the motivation to perform times skill times the capital to buy material, plant, and equipment yields value. The components are not additive because a missing component in the communications system causes all value to be lost.

In addition, $1 + 0 = 1$. In multiplication, $1 \times 0 = 0$. If you have knowledge but no motivation, you have no result. Likewise, if you have any missing element, skill or capital, your result is essentially zero. Most small businesses fail not because they lack knowledge or motivation or even the skill to run a small enterprise. They fail because they run out of capital. All elements, not three out of four, are necessary for success.

When data are ignored or information is stifled or used erroneously, the organization suffers. The company's information system is analogous to the circulatory system of the human body. It carries nutrients through the arteries of the organization in the form of data points. The various systems absorb and utilize the data, discarding what becomes useless, releasing it back into the circulatory system, which returns the residue of operations through the veins to be excreted or recycled and converted once again into nutrients of current value. When valid useful information is blocked, the system goes into a form of cardiac arrest.

Information Technology

The speed of change that we are experiencing today could never have happened without the recent advances in information technology. By putting more information literally at our fingertips and in front of our eyes, we can respond more quickly. The faster we respond, the faster things change. The volume of information thrust upon us at every moment of our lives from the second we wake up until we retire at night, along with the rate of change and exchange, are combining at such speed and with such force that many people are on overload. Think back to what business was like in the 1960s, if you were around. What type of information was available? How often was there a fundamental change in your company's products and services? If you weren't there, let me tell you that the quantity and movement of information then, compared to now, were comparable to the difference between a box turtle and a charging bull elephant. Management's responsibility is to filter the incoming data, convert them into useful information, and transmit that information to its employees in forms they can comprehend and apply. This is called knowledge, and, as we saw above, knowledge is power.

Besides speed there are also economies. Information technology and processing capability put into the hands of the employee yield some surprising results.

At Mellon Bank in Pittsburgh the company was suffering from the region's economic downturn of the 1980s. Concurrently, its health care costs were rising at an annual double-digit rate into the early 1990s. Finally, in 1993 the bank decided to introduce managed care.

This required employees to reenroll and to make some choices about their health care coverage. Traditionally, this had been a time-consuming, expensive proposition for the 22,000-employee firm. It was decided to use an interactive self-enrollment process. This process, called PRESS (Press and Response Enrollment Selection System), allowed employees to make enrollment decisions and enter their selections via a touch-tone telephone system open twenty-four hours a day during the enrollment period. The underlying software program immediately verified the enrollment and updated the system. The results of the enrollment project were as follows:

- ❑ Individual enrollment time was reduced from an average four and a half minutes to two minutes and forty-five seconds.
- ❑ The error rate under self-enrollment dropped from 12 percent to 2.5 percent.
- ❑ Because 84 percent of the employees chose this enrollment method, paper usage was reduced by 30,000 pieces and the need for several temporary clerical employees to process paper was eliminated.
- ❑ The new managed care initiative reduced the rate of increase in health care costs from 17 percent to 5 percent, representing a cost avoidance of about $6,800,000.

In addition, to improve employee communications in general, Mellon established a Customer Service Center for employees who had problems or questions. Typically, these types of inquiries go first to the supervisor and then to a local employee relations person. But finding the right person with the requisite knowledge is not always a slam dunk.

With the CSC, an employee can pick up an internal phone and dial 6-HR4U and be connected to the center, which is staffed by specially trained personnel. The purported benefits are that within thirty seconds of dialing the employee is connected to a qualified person capable of answering the inquiry; line managers and supervisors can get consistent and up-to-date information; and senior management has constant feedback on the issues and concerns of its employees. During its first year of operation the CSC received 125,000 calls. Of all incoming calls, 85 percent were answered within thirty seconds. The average time spent on the phone to provide an answer was ninety seconds. And 92 percent of all inquiries and problems were resolved on the first call.

Knowing How to Use the Data

Given all the books about management swamping the stores, there are remarkably few that deal with employee communications. Most of what has been written is prescriptive and focused on emerging information technology. Although most writers give a paragraph to "thou shalt communicate," hardly anyone tells us what to do or how we should do it. Therefore, it is not surprising that most companies do not do a great job with respect to this complex human activity.

The central problem is pointed out by Peter Drucker.[1] While acknowledging that many executives are now computer-literate, he claims that most are still information-illiterate. He describes this as knowing how to get data but not knowing how to use what emerges. I encounter this every day when I train managers on performance measurement. Often they don't know what information they need to do their jobs more effectively. They tend to take what the system gives them or complain that they don't have enough data to do their jobs. But the problem is not quantity; it is definition. They should be asking and answering these questions:

What data do I need, at what times, and in what forms?
What I should be communicating to others?
What are the media and formats I should be using for different audiences?

An outgoing management report is more than data. It is an opportunity to influence as well as to inform. This means it is a selling situation. Selling demands knowing the customer and communicating with him or her in a format and on a time basis that are suitable.

Three Types of Information

We need both data and skills if we want to be effective communicators. These requirements fall into three categories.

Conditional Information

Everyone needs information about their health. Companies too need frequent information on the state of their health. Cash flow, inventory levels, sales, morale, and efficiency level data are necessary. These are fundamental cost, time, quantity, and quality data that are equivalent to knowing one's pulse, temperature, and blood pressure. When they vary from an expected range, it is a sign of impending organizational illness. Statistical process control is the operation manager's thermometer. Just as you take aspirin to bring down a high temperature, so you need to have process remedies for deviations from basic operating parameters.

Competence Information

Companies are now talking competence. At this level we are thinking about corporate competence. There are three key competencies that every organization needs today: information, innovation, and inspiration competence.

To start strategic planning and later to manage organizations you have to know what type of data you need, how to get it, how to process it, and how to interpret it. This, I find, is the area of greatest potential improvement. Very few people know how to find patterns and connections or to see the underlying, half-hidden trends that pattern perception yields. At the corporate level, human competence should be defined in strategic terms. Motorola's business/technical skills, relationship management, and analytic capability are a good example.

The second macro competence is innovation. Innovation helps keep a company from disappearing by pushing it toward the leading edge of its technology. This competence is usually one of the four or five Balanced Scorecard factors that increasingly are being adopted. One way to evaluate innovation competence is by the amount of income accruing from new versus old products. As an example, at Hewlett-Packard more than 50 percent of current sales are from products that have been on the market less than three years. Psychologist Rosabeth Moss Kanter states that one of the most common roadblocks to innovation is poor communication across departments.[2] To overcome this, Hewlett-Packard goes to extraordinary lengths to encourage face-to-face information sharing on a timely basis. Even though Kanter's research is from the early 1980s, the problem seems very much alive today in some companies. The BHAMs have applied massive, multidirectional communications of their base values and culture up through activity such as partnering and collaboration.

The third macro competence, one that is often addressed in a very haphazard, after-the-horse-is-out-of-the-barn fashion, is inspiration. Top management must be capable of capturing the hearts and minds of the people if it wants an above-average company. GE's Jack Welch put it very well when he said:

> *"Any company that's going to make it in the '90s and beyond has got to find a way to engage the mind of every single employee. If you're not thinking all the time about making every person more valuable, you don't have a chance."*

The only thing I would add is that we also need to capture the *spirit,* or the hearts, of people if we want to survive the bad as well as the good times.

Production Information

Production, as I use the term, includes productivity, quality, and service levels. Conditional information tells you the financial state of your corporate health. Production information tells you how you got to that level and predicts how you might look and feel tomorrow. Each department should be monitoring and feeding back to its staff the current and projected production levels against their targets. Top management needs to monitor total system productivity. Recently, economic value analysis (EVA) has been growing in popularity as a total system measure. EVA is net operating profit after tax less the cost of capital. This is the type of metric that needs to be tracked at the top of the system.

In addition, in the new world of intellectual capital, we need data on the productivity of the human and information resources. At the Saratoga Institute we monitor human investment ratio (HIR) for about twenty industries. HIR takes total sales and service revenue, subtracts all nonhuman costs (everything but pay and benefits), and divides the result by pay and benefits. This yields a ratio of dollars spent on people to pretax net income.

Once management has results for its own company, it is then useful to benchmark the industry leaders. Putting this type of macro data on display, with a thorough explanation of what it implies, can be very motivating to employees. Most people like to feel they are working for one of the industry leaders. While management might claim that the company is just that, there is more credibility to the claim when it is backed up with hard data simple enough for everyone to understand.

The Real Communications Hub: The Supervisor

When organizations talk about employee communications, the discussion and planning are usually centered on the media that will be used and the content or topics to be broadcast. But there are two other issues whose neglect often leads to draining much of the life out of the communication. The first is very important and frequently ignored. That is the receiver. How often have you heard anyone ask, "What do the employees want to know?" Management usually focuses on what *it* wants to share. The second issue is even more important because it is the crucial hub of communications. I'm not talking about the communications department or even the network technology. I'm talking about the supervisor. Unquestionably, the employee's immediate supervisor has more influence over whether or not a communication passes through the system accurately than does anyone or anything else.

USAA FINDS THE COMMUNICATIONS KEY

United Services Automobile Association, headquartered in San Antonio, was founded in 1922 to provide automobile insurance for U.S.

Army officers. It has grown until today it is the only insurance company to operate in all fifty states. USAA also provides a full range of life and accident insurance, banking and mutual fund services, and a travel service. Run largely by retired military officers, the company has always had a reputation for efficiency and service. Its culture was rather paternalistic and self-contained. A central feature of the company has been its attention to the welfare of its 17,000 employees. Employees had a sense of being in the womb and very secure. To ensure security, base pay was adjusted annually to keep up with the cost of living index. Annual salary increases were virtually guaranteed. Everyone was treated as an individual—to the point where 2,500 job descriptions had been developed.

In the early 1990s, it became clear that, despite the company's financial success, things had to change. Even though customer service was excellent, it couldn't continue at the same level given the changes in the marketplace. This planned change was fully launched in 1994 by what top management described as "shared responsibility for our employability." What this means is that the company could no longer provide the type of security it had offered in the past. The competition, regulations and deregulation, evolving customer requirements, new opportunities, and all the rest of the shifting characteristics of the financial marketplace made security a function solely of performance. Longevity and attendance were no longer guarantees of employment. This was real culture change.

Management opted for a proactive approach. Rather than put out the word and wait for people to react to the change, top management decided to orchestrate it. The change was to be driven by a massive communications program. USAA had previously learned two things about employee communications. The first was that you can never communicate too much. Particularly in times of change and uncertainty, communicating is a constant activity. It is not a program; it is an inherent part of daily management. Accordingly, the company had made heavy investments in state-of-the-art communications technology, which was in constant use. Besides the typical corporate print media, there is an internal e-mail system for instantaneous communications. The company also produces a weekly television program that is transmitted across the country to all employees.

The second insight was even more important. Management had learned through previous communications research, described below, that the key to the change was going to be the supervisor-employee exchange. Each person's immediate supervisor, no matter what the level, is the most important channel and medium of communication.

Prior to the launching of the culture change, the company had inaugurated an intensive management communications training program. All supervisors and managers went through a series of communications training programs. They were taught about their role as communicators and keepers of the flame. They were also trained in effective communication techniques. This training was just the beginning. Top management publicly reinforced their role and responsibility.

The message to all employees from Admiral Hacker, chief administrative officer, stated that supervisors and managers at all levels were the key to successful communication and management of the change. They had to carry the word that while systems were going to change, the core values of USAA were not. Management was still dedicated to the individual, but now individuals had to help themselves develop. The demands of the market meant that no one could simply occupy a desk. Each employee from bottom to top had to be constantly learning, improving, and contributing if the company was to maintain its competitive advantages.

A major aspect of the change was the redesign of the compensation system. Great pains were taken to communicate to all employees why the pay system had to change and how the new program would function. In lieu of COLA increases and matter-of-fact annual "merit" increases, there would now be more of a direct linkage between pay and performance. This is easy to say, and practically every company currently proclaims it. But USAA backed up its rhetoric with system changes that touched every employee. First, the 2,500 job descriptions were reduced to about 200. This greatly simplified the pay structure. Then, early in 1996, the internally driven pay grade system was eliminated. It was replaced by a market-referenced guide with four broad bands of pay. This system will be adjusted annually on the basis of competitive conditions. A performance bonus plan was designed with individual, business unit, and corporate bonus potential.

All supervisory personnel received intensive training in how to communicate the intricacies of the system and plan changes. They were taught not only how to put the information out but also how to deal with questions and reactions that would probably be somewhat emotional and perhaps even distrustful. The supervisory communications effort was backed up with employee surveys, focus groups, and individual interviews. Constant testing for feedback on understanding and feelings went on. Predictably, the volume of feedback was overwhelming. Contrary to some views of the work force, it is not a monolith. When you say something to 17,000 people, you have to be prepared to deal with 17,000 reactions. The managers and the human resource staff developed a partnership to cope with the feedback implosion.

Besides pay changes, there was a strong emphasis placed on employee development. Management committed extra resources and developed a new function to support the employees' growth. The employee development operation was expanded and charged with education and training and the design of a work force development center. The message carried by the supervisors was that management was providing the tools of self-development. Employees were expected to get involved in their own growth. A map of USAA's intended growth path was communicated to everyone. And everyone was told that there were certain skill packages needed from each functional area to support the corporate plan.

Nor were managers neglected. They too are supervisors of people. They were supported with a new leadership development program and a 360-degree appraisal system. This helped them learn what they needed as individuals to grow with the company. Finally, an ethics program was instituted, based on a benchmarking project that covered twenty-four companies (twelve financial corporations and twelve other service and manufacturing firms). This was another example of management's proactive attitude toward the changes that had to be anticipated and dealt with. While there had been no ethical problems in the company up to then, the top executive team wanted to make sure that the culture change would not leave the company vulnerable to any in the future. Big change causes pressure and pressure stimulates some people to react by cutting corners. This was not acceptable and therefore had to be preempted.

To keep everyone informed of the progress of the change, USAA has invested heavily in the latest communications technology. Weekly employee communications programs are broadcast to all employees over its satellite television network. Videotapes of the programs are available for those who cannot view the live program. Print media include weekly and monthly newsletters, and employee surveys are a regular event. In short, management threw every communications medium possible into the battle. Even with this massive investment, their assessment is that they didn't do too much.

USAA's strategic approach to communicating the culture change was supported by the findings of a research project carried out two decades earlier.

In the early 1970s a project in a major West Coast bank focused on employee communications from the bottom up.[3] Fourteen hundred people at all levels were instructed to deal with three information variables in the following manner:

1. Rank and rate the level of interest you have in the main topics that management tends to communicate. They are: job performance, career opportunity, personnel policies, work and organizational change, daily operations, company finances, company strategy and plans, competitor actions, and general employee news.

2. Rank-order who you want to communicate each of these topics to you: (a) your supervisor; (b) a senior division officer; (c) a senior staff professional; (d) the top corporate officer.

3. Rank-order the method you prefer for each of the above topics: (a) face-to-face; (b) a group meeting; (c) company memos or newsletters; (d) a posted notice.

Overwhelmingly, on the topics of greatest interest, the supervisor was the hands-down first choice as the communicator. The most preferred method was face-to-face. No other form or person even came close.

In order of importance, the respondents placed job performance and career opportunity far above all other topics as the most important. Next came information regarding personnel policies on pay and benefits. This was followed by a grouping of information on work and organizational change, daily operations, company plans, and profitability. Finally, for most people, information on the competition and general company news (anniversaries, personal news, social and recreational items) were of least interest.

Subsequent applications of that questionnaire yielded the same results. No difference was found when the data were sorted by sex, race, or job level. There were only two differences uncovered. One was by age group. Persons who were nearing retirement had no interest in career opportunities or in any other information regarding the future except for retiree benefits. The other was by function. There were differences between line and staff functions on news of the competition. Line people rated that higher than staff employees did. This was probably because the line was more in touch with the marketplace. Every subsequent application over a four-year period reinforced the initial conclusion that the supervisor is the cornerstone of corporate-employee communications.

These findings reinforce statements made by Peter Drucker in his seminal work, *The Practice of Management.* Drucker lists communications as one of the five basic operations in the work of a manager.

> *"He does it [makes a team out of people] through constant communication, both from the manager to the subordinate and from the subordinate to the manager."*[4]

Notice the word *constant.* Communication is not an afterthought. It is the very heart of managing. This is a key differentiator between the BHAMs and The Rest.

Types of Communications

Lavish Communications

In *Leadership Is an Art,* Max Dupree, former CEO of the Herman Miller Company, claims that *lavish communications* are necessary for the intelligent organization.[5] He offers his own company as an example. He kept employees informed and up to date with the few types of information shown in Figure 5-2.

In BHAM companies we see how information leads to trust and empowerment. It is not reasonable to expect employees to trust management when management is stingy with information.

Figure 5-2. Topics communicated to all employees.

- Financial results in detail
- Current productivity measures
- Customers' needs and wishes
- Market share and news about the competition
- Strategies of the organization
- How these strategies relate to local priorities
- Quality statistics
- Customer satisfaction statistics
- New products and services in development
- Pollution, waste, and the cost of energy use

How would you feel if you didn't know what was going on? Especially in today's world of revolutionary change, information is the greatest weapon.

Building Trust in Bad Times

There is no question that one of the most critical times for communicating with employees is during periods of hardship. When things are going badly, people feel it. Lack of communication at this time is like throwing fuel on the fire. The grapevine then becomes the communications channel, and most of the time the news emanating from it is both negative and wrong.

Financial Information Trust is a typical small company in the heartland of America. It employs about 275 people in Des Moines, Iowa. It was founded in 1978 by a group of savings and loan institutions to provide data processing services to the group. When the fuzz hit the fan in the S&L industry, FIT was forced to downsize. In the first rounds, each layoff spread a wave of panic throughout the work force because it came without warning. This caused the survivors to look constantly over their shoulders for the next bad news. Productivity dropped, customer service fell off, and involuntary turnover among key staff doubled. The fear of the unknown took over.

A change in management brought a new communications policy. All functional heads were required to review their expected staff needs three months into the future. If a reduction in force was inevitable owing to a declining customer base, those employees who were to be affected were taken aside and told. But their identity was not disclosed to others lest they be stigmatized. Then, all employees were told that another downsizing was coming and that the affected personnel had already been notified. This reduced anxiety. Involuntary terminations dropped off. Productivity and morale increased, and customer satisfaction achieved record highs. Trust had been reestablished through open and honest communication of bad news. Those affected also had more time to find other positions within the company or to prepare their job search.

Many managers believe that people cannot handle bad news rationally. This is not true. Time and again the evidence shows that people know how to deal with adversity because it is a part of everyone's life. Most people, when frankly given full information, handle it well. When we talk about withholding information, we describe it as "keeping people in the dark." The worst fear is the fear of the unknown. Beyond the issue of nondisclosure and blackout periods, management should communicate everything it possibly can. When you hold back, you don't protect people; rather, you send a message of lack of respect and distrust.

Sharing the Good News

In today's lean and mean environment in which everyone has to do more with less, issues like absenteeism can have a significant effect on production targets. There are many ways to stimulate high attendance. One way to operate is to punish absenteeism that goes beyond a certain level. The only problem with punishment is that in time the person being punished becomes immune and it takes increasingly stronger doses to obtain the desired response.

There is ample evidence among the BHAMs that positive reinforcement is a more effective treatment than punishment is for absenteeism.

Sunbeam Plastics, with plants in Evansville and Princeton, Indiana, makes plastic closure systems. Its largest business is those childproof screw-on caps that no adult can open. Because the company must operate at a very high level of productivity it needs all its employees on the job all the time. To encourage this, Sunbeam uses a comprehensive strategy of recognition programs and flexible work schedules.

When employees qualify for an award based on perfect attendance and no tardiness for six months, they receive a nonmonetary award. To make the awards memorable, these are given out during the employees' shift in front of their peers. This is augmented with an honor roll published in the company newspaper, which is mailed to the employees' homes. Workers with perfect attendance for short time periods receive simple awards such as caps or T-shirts. As attendance continues unbroken, the value of the award goes up. One person with a long record of perfect attendance received a weekend trip for himself and his spouse plus eight hours worth of holiday pay. Another received a VCR for eleven unbroken years.

Other recognition programs designate people as "Hero" or "Star" for extraordinary performance. This program is run by the employees for their peers. Awards, again, are simple and are given out at shift meetings and published in the company paper. This program needs some monitoring to ensure the quality of the performance being recognized. Along with the Hero and Star programs is a suggestion system that is run by representatives from the different functional areas. They are the Suggestion Evaluation Team and rule on all awards.

The cumulative result of these recognition programs at Sunbeam is an absence rate 50 percent lower than the industry average. It has also helped with employee retention and work performance. Scrap rate dropped from 5.6 percent to 2 percent, and downtime for production changeover dropped from 8 to 4.8 hours. On-time shipment improved 27 percent over the last two years recorded.

Rewarding what you do want takes fewer resources and achieves better results than punishing what you don't want.

Sharing Information Across Borders

Gifford and Elizabeth Pinchot claim that both the marketplace and organizational life have become so complex and multidimensional that there is no way of utilizing traditional chains of command to communicate in a timely and effective manner.[6] Integration must be achieved, and this is best done through peer-level, cross-organizational communications. Because every important process crosses several organizational boundaries, vertical communications can never keep up.

These complexity and speed dimensions are the drivers of collaboration, partnering, and the forging of alliances. By building a collective intelligence you can obtain more information faster, learn faster, and respond faster. With speed being a differentiating force into the foreseeable future, we must have all relevant information available for as many people as possible at all times. Sharing of information across borders has the benefit of facilitating useful feedback, of helping employees understand the basis of managerial decisions, of stimulating improvement, and of recognizing achievement. Nothing so empowers people, builds trust, and recaptures lost loyalty as sharing of a wide range of information on a regular basis.

Widening Your Competitive Advantage

The most dramatic driver of rapid, large-scale change is interpersonal communications supported by information technology. Nicholas Imparato and Oren Harari build their model of the smart organization, the kind necessary for "jumping the curve," around communications. They present four initiatives[7] that make aggressive use of information technology:

1. Leverage knowledge across the organization.
2. Accelerate the development of collaborative work both within and outside the company.
3. Prioritize efforts that lead to mass customization, slenderized marketing, and individualized customer sets (by knowing customers and integrating strategies).
4. Liberate people from the constraints of the paper-dependent environment.

Our work in gaining competitive advantage relies on communicating what can and must be. Since systems drive behavior, the old unwanted or the new desired behavior, it makes sense to rework our systems. Either the old modified or the newly designed system is an implicit communicator. It tells us exactly what are the preferred behaviors—from which door to enter to which way to turn and what to do when we get inside.

Communication in the Next Millennium

If knowledge is the key resource of the future, then communication is the vehicle. In *Workplace 2000*, Joseph H. Boyett and Henry P. Conn provide a list of questions that the employee of the future must be able to answer if he or she is to add value.[8] Figure 5-3

Figure 5-3. Employee information requirements in the twenty-first century.

---

1. What makes your company unique? How does it differentiate itself from its competitors?
2. Who are your company's major competitors?
3. What are your company's strengths and weaknesses versus its major competitors?
4. How do your company's costs for producing goods and services compare to those of your company's major competitors?
5. How is your company performing in respect to sales and profits?
6. Who are your company's major or target customers? What types of needs or expectations do these customers have that your company is trying to satisfy? How satisfied are these customers with your company's perform-ance in meeting their needs or expectations?
7. What is your company's business strategy? What are the key objectives for your company over the next one to five years?
8. What is the role of your work group in helping your company to imple-ment its business strategy?
9. What are the key goals/objectives for your work group over the next one to five years? How do these goals/objectives support your company's business strategy?
10. What are the key measures of performance for your work group?
11. What is the current performance of your work group on these key mea-sures?
12. What projects does your work group have underway to improve perform-ance on these measures?

Source: "Future Information Sharing," from *Workplace 2000* by Joseph H. Boyett and Henry P. Conn. Copyright © 1991 by Joseph H. Boyett and Henry P. Conn. Used by permission of Dutton Signet, a division of Penguin Books USA Inc.

shows what the authors think the twenty-first-century employee will be required to know. They point out that currently most companies do not share much of this information. Their message is that you can't expect people to go beyond merely doing their job to adding value so long as they are operating in a vacuum. If knowledge is power, then power is motivating.

BHAM Lesson: *You can't communicate too much.*

Employee Viewpoint Survey

The final evaluators of your employee communications are the receivers (i.e., your employees). If you want to know how effective your communications system is, ask the people who are most affected by it. The topics listed in the questionnaire in Figure 5-4 are the basic topics that most companies communicate to their employees. Their responses tell you what is most and least important to them, who they want to deliver the message on each topic, the medium they most prefer, and how satisfied they are with the current quality and quantity of information you are trying to communicate.

Summary

Communication is the method that we use to leverage intellectual capital. To be valuable, data and information have to be mobile. People and information have to interact or nothing happens. Management's job is to guide the acquisition, conversion, and distribution of information. Communication is not an afterthought. It is a core task. Communication is also a critical variable in partnerships, teamwork, alliances, and future strategic planning.

The management of communications begins with a strategy and a belief in the ability of people to handle information—both good news and bad. Even though communication is the most pervasive of human activities, special skills are required by both the sender and the receiver. The skills are cognitive, social, and technical in nature. When accurate information is effectively transmitted, the receiver is not only more knowledgeable but also more trusting of the sender. This sense of trust and security empowers the re-

(text continues on page 112)

Figure 5-4. Survey of employees' attitudes toward company communications.

___

1. Rank and rate your level of importance and interest in the following topics:

   Column A. Rank order from 1 (high) to 10 (low) your *priority* of importance of the topics, one versus the other.
   Column B. Rate from 1 (high) to 5 (low) your level of interest in *each* topic.

   A   B

   _____   Your career opportunities   _____
   _____   Changes in the company's structure   _____
   _____   Company strategy, plans, and objectives   _____
   _____   Company values and vision   _____
   _____   Company finances (profitability)   _____
   _____   News about the company's competitors   _____
   _____   Daily operational matters (schedules,   _____
               procedures)
   _____   General company news (social and   _____
               recreational)
   _____   Your job performance (self and/or team)   _____
   _____   Personnel policies (pay, benefits, etc.)   _____

2. For each topic, write in the number of the person you would most prefer to communicate the topic to you.

   1. Your supervisor
   2. Senior manager from your division
   3. The CEO
   4. Staff department personnel or manager

   _____   Your career opportunities
   _____   Changes in the company's structure
   _____   Company strategy, plans, and objectives
   _____   Company values and vision
   _____   Company finances (profitability)
   _____   News about the company's competitors
   _____   Daily operational matters (schedules, procedures)
   _____   General company news (social and recreational)
   _____   Your job performance (self and/or team)
   _____   Personnel policies (pay, benefits, etc.)

3. For each topic, write in the number of the method you most prefer for having that information conveyed to you in Column A. In Column B, write in the number of the method you least prefer for that topic.

   1. Face to face in a personal meeting
   2. Orally in a group meeting
   3. Posted on a bulletin board or your workstation screen
   4. Written in a company newsletter or magazine
   5. Via closed-circuit television or on videotape (if available)

A = Most   B = Least

A	Topic	B
_____	Your career opportunities	_____
_____	Changes in the company's structure	_____
_____	Company strategy, plans, and objectives	_____
_____	Company values and vision	_____
_____	Company finances (profitability)	_____
_____	News about the company's competitors	_____
_____	Daily operational matters (schedules, procedures)	_____
_____	General company news (social and recreational)	_____
_____	Your job performance (self and/or team)	_____
_____	Personnel policies (pay, benefits, etc.)	_____

4. Rate from 1 (high) to 5 (low) how satisfied you are with the (A) quality and (B) quantity of the information you are receiving now on each topic (regardless of whether you agree with or like the statements made).

A = Quality   B = Quantity

A	Topic	B
_____	Your career opportunities	_____
_____	Changes in the company's structure	_____
_____	Company strategy, plans, and objectives	_____
_____	Company values and vision	_____
_____	Company finances (profitability)	_____
_____	News about the company's competitors	_____
_____	Daily operational matters (schedules, procedures)	_____
_____	General company news (social and recreational)	_____
_____	Your job performance (self and/or team)	_____
_____	Personnel policies (pay, benefits, etc.)	_____

ceiver. If motivation is stimulated and the skills are employed, the organization has a good chance of achieving the results it desires.

Advances in information technology have been a major factor in speeding us from the industrial to the information world. Technology not only gives capability, it also brings stressful demands. The faster we can transmit information, the faster we have to react. At this point we are better at transmitting than at reacting. Or even anticipating. Drucker points out our relative ineptitude with information by claiming that we know how to get it but not how to use it. We have not trained people on data pattern recognition. They don't see relationships across data points. There are three types of information: conditional, competence, and production. The first type tells the basic state of health of the organization. The second covers the skills needed to interact effectively. The third describes how effectively we are carrying out our work. The second and third can be employed as leading indicators.

The central figure in organizational communications is the supervisor. No matter what the topic is, people tend to ask their supervisor for an interpretation and a reaction. Field and academic research all points to the fact that people want to know how well they are doing and what is coming next. They trust their supervisor to give them that intelligence.

Companies that have pursued vigorous communications programs have been rewarded with low absenteeism, low turnover, and high productivity. There are many vehicles for communicating recognition of exceptional performance. Most of them are not costly, but they do take time and insight to select and apply in an effective manner.

References

1. Peter Drucker, *Managing in a Time of Great Change* (New York: Dutton, 1995).
2. Rosabeth Kanter, *The Change Masters* (New York: Simon & Schuster, 1983), pp. 160–162.
3. Jac Fitz-enz, unpublished doctoral dissertation, University of Southern California, 1974.

4. Peter Drucker, *The Practice of Management* (New York: Harper and Row, 1954), p. 344.
5. Max Dupree, *Leadership Is an Art* (New York: Doubleday, 1989), p. 147.
6. Gifford Pinchot and Elizabeth Pinchot, *The End of Bureaucracy and the Rise of the Intelligent Organization* (San Francisco: Berrett-Koehler Publishers, 1994), p. 38.
7. Nicholas Imparato and Oren Harari, *Jumping the Curve* (San Francisco: Jossey-Bass, 1994), pp. 155–182.
8. Joseph H. Boyett and Henry P. Conn, *Workplace 2000* (New York: Dutton 1991).

6

Partnering
With Stakeholders

*How the Best Build Inside and
Outside Relationships That
Leverage Resources for
Competitive Advantage*

One of the more notable trends in management theory during the
1990s has been the emphasis on relationships. The subject first attracted attention with Regis McKenna's *Relationship Marketing*.[1] His
notion was that changing times called for a more effective way to
market products and that this could be achieved through establishing a relationship with customers at a level that was much closer
or more intense than it had been in the past. The key to success
was to be human interaction along with product development. Mc-
Kenna advocated alliances even among competitors, citing a 1984
quotation from *Business Week*:

> *"For companies large and small, collaboration is the key to
> survival."*

This was a novel thought at the time. The well-publicized success of McKenna's clients, mostly electronic firms in California's

Silicon Valley, added credibility to his argument. Years later, that advice is more fitting than ever. Today, even more than in the past, business success is built primarily around human issues.

The collaboration concept has expanded from marketing to related functions such as product development. Managers are urged to develop relationships, now more commonly called alliances, with other firms. The rationale for this includes gaining knowledge of new technologies or manufacturing processes, speeding time to market, and strengthening one's market position. The new corporate buddy system has also spread to staff functions for one pragmatic reason: It works. Today, you can't pick up a newspaper or magazine without seeing several stories about alliances either forming or dissolving between and among groups of companies. The BHAMs must have read and applied the idea because partnering is a strong characteristic of their operations.

The Paradox of American Individualism

In a way, the movement toward collaboration through partnerships and alliances goes against the concepts of individualism and competition. It's another paradox. Citizens of the United States have long been noted for their individualism. It has been a source of pride for many of us. The cowboy is our national alter ego. Our attitude has long been "Every man for himself and the devil take the hindmost." Up to the 1980s, individualism was the cornerstone of our self-concept. We were the people who left the old country across the ocean to seek adventure and conquer the wilderness. We were the pioneers who opened the West and realized the promise of the New World. Then, for a variety of sociological, economic, and psychological reasons, that began to change. Today, the idea of individual responsibility never seems to enter the consciousness of many Yanks.

Paralleling that personal shift is the post–Civil War evolution of business practices. Stemming from the efforts of early industrialists to create monopolies and corner their markets, we developed a national paranoia regarding industrial power and collusion between companies. Shortly after the war, a number of high-profile cases revealed to the public how the industrial barons were doing their damnedest to lock up markets even at the expense of the customer or the country. Examples of this behavior are so numerous that a historian looking at the second half of the nineteenth century might think that monopolism was the primary goal of businessmen, and for many it probably was. All entrepreneurs and businesspeople want as large a share of a market as they can grab. Up to a point, there is nothing wrong with that. In the United States, this natural tendency was exacerbated by the frontier-busting, individualistic ethic of the country throughout the first 200 years of our history. However, by the 1880s, with the explosive national growth driven by the westward expansion, the power of large corporations became so great that a reaction naturally set in. In 1886, the American Federation of Labor was formed to give skilled laborers some power in dealing with excesses of management. The federal government responded, somewhat reluctantly, in 1890 with the passage of the Sherman Anti-Trust Act, outlawing monopolies and restraint of trade practices. That set the tone for intense business competition for the next eighty years.

When I first entered the electronics field in the mid-1970s, the attitude of the young Turks, who had ventured out to form their own companies, was blatant self-confidence and a self-reliance bordering on arrogance. Operating behind gross margins exceeding 60 percent, they thought themselves impervious to the vagaries of the marketplace. When the Japanese entered the semiconductor and components markets, and severely cut prices to capture market share, their tune changed. Within a decade the no longer quite so young, strong, or self-confident entrepreneurs turned to Washington for protection. Gradually, they learned that the federal government wasn't their salvation either.

The last nail in the coffin of individualism came with the corporate raiders of the 1980s. In their alleged attempts to "add value for the stockholder," they exhibited a level of greed and disregard for the commonwealth that was unparalleled since the days of the robber barons. The scandals stemming from their cold-blooded selfishness along with the savings and loan debacle demonstrated once again that there might be a better way to run businesses for the good of all. As these forces collided around 1990, executives began to look at how they might work together with allies and even competing firms for a common good. The BHAMs have made partnering a centerpiece of their operating style.

Teams, Partnerships, and Alliances

Some readers feel that teams, partnerships, and alliances are all the same thing. For the sake of clarity, you may want to consider how *The American Collegiate Dictionary* distinguishes them:

> **team:** *a number of persons associated in some joint action*
> **partner:** *a sharer or partaker, one associated with another or others as a principal or a contributor of capital in a business or a joint venture, usually sharing its risks and profits*
> **alliance:** *any joining of efforts or interests by persons, families, states, or organizations*

My experience is that these are distinctions among similar forms, like children within a family. I would differentiate these forms of collaboration on the basis of two criteria: scope and commitment. Partnerships typically deal with larger and longer-term issues than do teams. The line might be a fine one, but that is my observation. Partners tend to commit more of themselves than do members of teams. This is because the nature of the problem or task requires it. It could be that what were actually partnerships have been called teams. This may be only a semantic difference, but in my mind a partnership is much more than a team. I use the term *alliance* to describe a large partnership in which there are a number of players, whether they be individuals or organizational entities. Alliances are not always as intense as partnerships. The level of commitment seems higher in a partnership. These are the ways I've experienced the three types of collaboration. You may disagree, but at least we have a set of definitions to work from hereafter. As Humpty Dumpty said to Alice, "When *I* use a word, it means just what I choose it to mean—neither more nor less."[2]

Competing or Partnering Internally

In some companies, competition is as intense between internal functions as it is with outsiders. Many cultures promote internal competition as a way to stimulate the best ideas and efforts. It's a form of corporate Darwinism. This method works well for some product development projects and not so well for others. It's only a matter of preferred style.

A counterargument suggests that it is wasteful to consume your resources fighting with your colleagues. Given a sense of collective commitment, logic dictates and evidence suggests that the best ideas can be generated when two or more individuals are focused on the same goal. Why spend time and creative energy trying to outflank your brethren? All resources are focused on winning together rather than on defeating the group on the other side of the aisle. In an era of increasingly scarce resources, it makes sense to grow by sharing. A short story from my personal experience may help illustrate my point.

Many years ago I was called in by my boss, Bill Howell, an excellent human being to whom I am eternally grateful. He started the conversation by congratulating me on my accomplishments. After giving me a goodly amount of attaboys he said, "Jac, you need to understand one thing. When we win there is glory enough for everyone. But when we lose there are no heroes." I got it. He meant: "Get on the team and work with the rest of us instead of going off on your own to slay the dragon."

In an alliance, several people or functions decide that by working cooperatively and sharing resources they might learn faster or solve a problem faster with a better result than by working alone or on parallel courses. Alliances and partnerships are based on the same dynamic: human relationships. In this case the dynamic operates on the principle that each party brings something unique to the task. There is a small common base of knowledge and, in theory at least, a singular motivation. The relationship contributes additional skills to the task. Businesspeople have finally come to the realization that things get done only when human beings act. All systems, policies, strategies, and resources, except the human resource, are inert. That is, they are lifeless and contribute their value only when something outside themselves picks them up and uses them. It has become increasingly clear to most people that one of the most effective ways to operate is to gather people around a goal and stimulate their motivation to contribute to that goal. The more we apply relationship management in the form of partnerships, the more we will see the truth about effective performance.

New Structures, New Methods of Working Together

The plethora of process improvement tools—reengineering, TQM, and benchmarking—along with large-scale layoffs have changed the structures of many companies. What they often fail to change is the way people in the resulting structures work together. It's like automating an inefficient manual process. In order to make organizations function more effectively, management has to back up the restructuring with new operating forms and a sincere, visible commitment to the values that underlie them. In today's world, collaboration seems to make sense as a method of operation. A collaborative organization runs on several values, shown in Figure 6-1: integrity, respect for people, ownership, accountability, consensus, and recognition. Note that consensus does not imply that everyone in the organization agrees on every point. What it means is that there is consensus on what the collaboration is aiming to achieve.

The quid pro quo of collaboration is simple and unequivocal. Basically, it's the Golden Rule in action. Maybe there is nothing new. When I was in graduate school studying industrial psychology, I called my mother to tell her what I was doing. After my lengthy and esoteric description of personality theory and group dynamics, she brought me back to reality with a simple evaluation: "It seems like common sense to me," she said. Such is the foundation of collaboration. A partnership should operate on the following principles:

❑ If I act with integrity, you will trust me and want to work with me.
❑ If I respect you, you will respect me.
❑ If I give you ownership in the process by asking you to be a decision maker instead of a decision receiver, you will be motivated to achieve positive results.
❑ If I clarify your responsibility and make you accountable

Figure 6-1. Collaborative values.

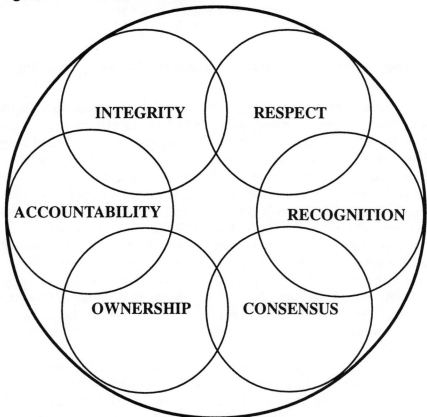

for your actions, you will strive to perform and in return
obtain job satisfaction.

❑ If everyone involved can go beyond merely accepting a decision to *buying into it*, we will all be committed.

❑ Finally, if I recognize your performance with some form of
reward, you will see that there is something in this for you
as well as for me and our companies.

These principles should be in effect no matter how intense or
stressful the partnership becomes. Maintaining one's principles in
times of stress is an admirable trait.

Partnering on a Traditional Problem

Often what top management looks upon as annoying little problems can become significant drains on operations farther down the line. The BHAMs seem to understand that the most cost-effective companies are those that analyze the full effect of all problems. In a previous chapter, we saw how Ames Rubber Company beat its quality problem by cutting turnover. If you have ever been concerned about the unwanted loss of key employees, the following case is a lesson in retention management.

Provident Bank of Maryland

Commercial banks have always had extremely high turnover rates in their teller lines. Annual rates of 40 percent and higher are not uncommon. This is not only costly in terms of continually having to replace tellers. It is also a pain in the neck for the many customers who like to establish a personal relationship with a teller. When it becomes too annoying, customers transfer their accounts to rival banks.

At Provident Bank of Maryland, founded in Baltimore in the 1880s, branch managers, operations officers, and recruiters became partners to reverse the turnover curve. The first thing they did was to develop a comprehensive strategy. It involved customer research, process change, linkage to operating needs, long-term planning, and commitment to a new method. It included five key elements:

1. The strategy started with research, something often missing in human resources work. The "partners" learned to predict the peak times of the year when tellers tended to leave for certain specific reasons. This pointed toward peak hiring periods that had to be planned for.

2. Because tellers needed both customer service and mathematical skills, Provident redesigned its screening process to test for them to make sure that it had only the best candidates in terms of both aptitudes. The combination of the first two steps ensured that there would be no fall-off in customer service at any time during the year.

3. The recruiters and the hiring supervisor negotiated clear specifications regarding skill requirements and the time needed to fill positions. This included job posting, use of preferred sources, unique needs, etc.

4. Because teller jobs are often dead ends, Provident developed and publicized a career path for novices from teller to financial services manager. This included a series of training and job experiences. Offering an opportunity to progress gave Provident a clear competitive advantage in the hiring market.

5. To anticipate peak loads, Provident established partnerships with the area's community service organizations, e.g., the Maryland Job Service Committee. Every Friday, the bank sent a listing of current and anticipated job openings to more than a dozen community organizations. In many cases, applications were back at the bank by the following Monday afternoon. With more candidates than they could use, they were able to organize a pool of qualified persons. This further cut down on the time it took to fill open positions.

The payoffs to the branch managers for partnering around a recruiting strategy helped Provident reduce the average time to fill teller jobs to just two days. By contrast, the average time to fill teller jobs on the eastern seaboard that year ranged from twelve to twenty-four days.

The Good News and Its Price

Because of the restructuring and delayering of organizations, the reduction of personnel, and the imposition of tight expense controls, organizational boundaries of necessity are becoming more permeable. This new permeability eases the flow of people and information across organizational borders. It makes it easier to acquire the knowledge needed quickly through alliances and partnerships. Suppliers, customers, and expert knowledge contributors in ever-growing numbers are taking part in management meetings dealing with planning, product design, personnel systems, and even budgeting. This introduction of outsiders into the central operation of the company is a phenomenon of the 1990s. With increasing frequency, even the union representative is invited into management meetings.

This good news comes at a price. If we are going to work through new structures, we have to learn how to do it effectively. Peter Senge cites the work of David Bohm on group dialogue.[3] Dialogue, according to Bohm, occurs when a group becomes open to the flow of a larger intelligence. That is the purpose of any group work (teams, partnerships, alliances): to create a larger collective intelligence. Bohm presents dialogue as a synthesis of the systems, holistic view of nature, and the interactions between our thinking models and our perceptions and actions. A full explanation of dialogue is beyond the scope of this book. I introduce it only to raise awareness of the different nature of partnering and to show what Bohm considers the three conditions necessary for dialogue, and hence effective partnering, to occur:

1. All participants must suspend their initial assumptions.
2. All participants must regard one another as colleagues.
3. There must be a facilitator who holds the context of dialogue (i.e., maintains the flow of dialogue versus argumentation).

The point of all this is that partnering is not the same as working alone or directing someone else's work. It requires a new perspective on the roles of the players. It also demands tolerance for conflicting opinions and a degree of patience that might sometimes try the patience of Job. But if handled well, the payoffs from partnering greatly exceed those from more traditional methods of project design and conduct.

Overcoming Competitive Disadvantage Through Partnering

TDS Computing Services, located in Madison, Wisconsin, was founded in 1976 to provide computer software and support to the telecommunications industry. Being based on state-of-the-art electronic technology, TDS/CS must stay on the cutting edge both in equipment and knowledge. This is a major challenge for a small company competing with the giants of the industry.

One of TDS/CS's commitments is to training. It sends every employee to a minimum of ten days of training annually. This cost the firm 3.6 percent of its total revenues in the last year surveyed. To manage this cost effectively, the company set up its own internal Learning Center. It also created a local partnership with other employers to fill classes where there were collective needs. For example, if TDS/CS has five employees who need database training, it notifies the partner companies and a full class is created. This reduces the cost per student of the training. At last count, eighteen joint classes were being offered. This simple strategy cut TDS/CS costs more than 20 percent annually and allowed the company to keep its people on the leading edge of technology.

A different kind of partnering was used to solve a problem in an insurance company's systems group. Systems needed to shrink by about 25 percent. They wanted to accomplish this in as positive a way as possible. In such cases, a package of salary and benefit extension is usually offered and anyone can take it. But in this situation, management wanted to keep certain key personnel. The human resources group strategized on how to send messages to certain people to stay. The plan was to have the human resources and systems management staffs rank the systems department professional staff. This is a tricky maneuver if you don't want to incur added costs from a forced layoff and unemployment compensation. After the ranking, all systems people were to be told where they ranked. There was no implied threat to the lower-ranked persons. Training got involved by teaching the management staff how to do this ethically, legally, and humanely. When the process was completed, most lower-rated performers took the package. Over 90 percent of those leaving came from the lowest quartile. The company kept almost everyone it wanted to, who were in the top quartile. Working together, systems and human resources saved money and succeeded in retaining the most highly valued staff members.

The Secondary Benefits of Partnering

Resource Leverage

One of the stronger arguments for forming partnerships is to leverage the resources of two or more persons or groups. The underlying purpose is to encourage managers to find ways for getting the most output from the least input. Resource management has two aspects: One is the allocation of resources across functions; the other is the multiplication of resources through various leveraging partnerships.

We spend most of our time on the administration, or allocation, of resources through budgeting and authorization meetings. We might find it more profitable to spend more of our time looking for ways to multiply the return on investment of those resources through partnering. It is more than possible that there is a higher incidence of partnering as a part of best human asset management among smaller firms, which are more resource-constrained than larger companies are. The larger firms, no matter how busy they are, have a critical mass of capital, people, and equipment that they can redistribute. Smaller companies know that they have to be creative because there is simply no way to obtain additional resources. Hamel and Prahalad offer a list of the features and potential benefits of resource leverage in Figure 6-2. Thoughtful consideration of the features should open your eyes to new applications of partnering.

Its Human Values

The BHAMs apparently see that partnering also has human as well as financial and technical values. Substantive contact with people

Figure 6-2. Features and potential benefits of resource leverage.

Feature	Benefit
Converging	Building consensus on strategic goals
Focusing	Specifying precise improvement goals
Targeting	Emphasizing high-value activities
Learning	Fully using the brainpower of every employee
Borrowing	Accessing resources of partners
Blending	Combining skills in new ways
Balancing	Securing critical complementary assets
Recycling	Reusing skills and resources
Co-opting	Finding common cause with others
Protecting	Shielding resources from competitors
Expediting	Minimizing time to pay back

Source: Gary Hamel and C. K. Prahalad, *Competing for the Future* (Boston: Harvard Business School Press, 1994), p. 175.

from other groups around a mutual or collective task helps accelerate human development and self-confidence. If one function can set aside its egocentrism under the principle of glory enough for all, great value can be obtained. When marketing pulls in finance, information services, human resources, and production people to work on an opportunity, everyone learns. Each group sees how the others perceive the problems of analysis, decision making, implementation, and evaluation. A new level of acceptance, if not appreciation, develops. Marketing sees that finance is not unreasonably stubborn. Production sees that human resources is also business-minded. Everyone sees that information people aren't the bottleneck.

When you begin to see and understand the viewpoints of others, you become more imaginative and creative. Your world is expanded. You have more pieces to play with and more potential ways to connect them. You come away from the partnership with a new, broader recognition of how things can work. You've gained new skills and a stronger sense of personal capability. On a parallel path, the experience also enhances your view of the organization's ability to succeed.

Being Part of Something Bigger

There are other psychological benefits of partnering. It is human nature to want to be part of something exciting that transcends ourselves. When you talk to people about what is really important to them, they always include their family and the organizations to which they belong, such as their company, church, school, neighborhood, or ethnic group. It's always more than just their personal security or success. For some, even their local sports team's prowess seems all-important. This is why the impact and value of a shared vision is so powerful. If you can convince people to identify with the corporate vision, you have more than their hands and minds; you have their spirit. Motivation is an inherent, emotional trait. Capture that and you have the person.

The Relationship Between Structure and Vision

To achieve commitment to the vision, management has to give evidence that it is serious about it. This is where the structural factors come into play. Management is required to set up the structure and systems needed to fulfill the vision. Structure is just as critical as the vision. To paraphrase Buckminster Fuller, if you want to change behavior, change the system. Peter Senge echoes Fuller on how structure influences behavior.[4]

> *"When placed in the same system, people, however different, tend to produce the same results."*

Several years ago I had an argument with the president of a subsidiary of a chemical company in the Midwest. He believed so much in the inherent goodness of people that he wouldn't pay any attention to systems. His view was that if you hired good people they would work together naturally to achieve the common goal. My contention was that they needed a structure within which to work out his vision. At the time, his company had a patent on its main product, which gave it essentially 90 percent of the market. They made money in spite of themselves. He ignored my views and went on to become CEO of the parent company. Two years after the patent protection ran out, his former group was in deep trouble because it had no framework to guide it.

Structures and systems can be physical, organizational, or relational. Each of them influences our perceptions and subsequent behaviors. I described in Chapter 4 how systems drive behavior and how behavior produces results. By introducing alliances and partnerships as a way of doing business, we move people to work together in new ways. These collaborative forms produce results that are larger than themselves or their department. This is what makes it exciting.

PARTNERSHIP TO THE RESCUE

A medical center director faced the prospect of having to merge, sell, or close his facility. Just about every aspect of his 3,000-employee, multisite medical complex was in trouble. Operational and administrative costs were rising and were seemingly out of control. Patient care was nowhere near acceptable standards. In fact, it was so bad that local, referring physicians were becoming concerned about the welfare of their patients. The staff's morale was somewhere between indifferent and combative. In short, as the director looked ahead there seemed to be a large light at the end of the tunnel and it clearly was a locomotive approaching at high speed.

At the time the company was operating in the red, and no one was willing to take the blame. There was defensiveness and finger pointing rather than commitment to a solution. On the human side, morale was at ground level and patient satisfaction scores were abominably low. Departing patients were given survey forms to evaluate the medical staff's performance. They weren't at all happy.

In a last attempt to salvage the center, the director brought in his top team and presented the problem. It was high noon and time to act or get out of town. After a long and agonizing discussion, it was decided that there were a few critical issues which, if resolved, might turn the tide. Two basic goals were established: (1) Turn the company around financially through better fiscal management and employee commitment, and (2) treat the patients better.

Group members pledged their respective forces to the strategy and to a list of key tasks and objectives. Cross-functional partnerships were formed and work began. The next year was one of great agony and frustration for many managers and supervisors. They were learning while burning. Trial and error taught them how to put aside their personal concerns and commit themselves to a partnership around the survival challenge. Partnerships occurred at two levels. One was corporate, where everyone was asked to join the effort to save the enterprise. The other was at the departmental level, where people from areas such as nursing, the labs, finance, guest relations, human resources, maintenance, and security joined one tactical partnership or another.

Within twenty-four months of the launch of the partnership, the financial situation had turned around. One might say it was unbelievable. From a bath of red ink, the center blew through the top of a challenging profit goal. On the patient side, survey satisfaction scores rose from a dangerously low 40 percent to 89 percent, putting the center above the ninetieth percentile of hospitals nationwide. It might be argued that any institution in a similar condition could do nothing but get better. But this is only partially true. It might have failed to solve its problems, merged, or gone out of business, as many health care facilities have done in the past decade. Alternatively, it might have limped along with some improvement stimulated only by employees' fear of losing their jobs. But it is undeniable that such a dramatic recovery and relaunch was the by-product of a commitment to partnering across functions. The people owned the problem and became partners in solving it.

Big Goals, Culture, and Partnering

Many of those we revere as the best companies have faced the bet-your-company project at some point in their histories. These projects required a high level of commitment throughout the organization. Such goals naturally enlist people from all parts of the enterprise, leading to the forming of many partnerships. The make-or-break projects demand total commitment and the highest levels of alliance making. If the company is going to realize the really big goals, it must leverage its resources through partnership management.

In describing the adaptive cultures that successfully reform themselves, Ralph Kilmann and his colleagues list the traits that permit companies to deal with unexpected or new challenges:[5]

❑ Willingness to take risks
❑ Trusting fellow employees
❑ Being proactive
❑ Being supportive
❑ Having a shared confidence
❑ Widespread enthusiasm
❑ Desire to do whatever it takes
❑ Receptivity to change and innovation

Many of these attributes are also requirements for big goal achievement and partnering. People don't take on big goals or partner effectively if they don't trust, aren't supportive, have little confidence or enthusiasm, and aren't willing to commit themselves to doing what it takes to be successful. It is clear that partnering is a hallmark of adaptive cultures.

John P. Kotter provides counterexamples to emphasize the point.[6] In summing up the research on adaptive cultures from the other side, he states that nonadaptive cultures are usually very bureaucratic and driven by self-interest. People are reactive, risk-adverse, and not very creative. Information does not flow easily and the emphasis is on control. Clearly, this is not an environment in which partnerships are condoned, suggested, or successful.

In a final example, Nicholas Imparato and Oren Harari talk about destabilizing forces that are driving many older managers crazy.[7] Raised in an era of stability and with a homogeneous work force, they now find themselves dealing with problems they never imagined. The two most obvious are racial and gender diversity and the restructuring of organizations. Instead of having the familiar chain of command and relationships built over the years with golfing buddies, today's managers have to organize new multiethnic and dual-gender work groups. The hope is that they learn to trade in their traditional command-and-control model for openness and knowledge sharing. Sharing includes internal and external groups that come and go. The organizations that are learning to rally people with diverse knowledge and skills into rapid response teams are winning the battle. Mobility, responsiveness to market changes, and innovation call for groupware, cross-functional alliances, and blurred boundaries. The BHAMs seem to be not only comfortable with this but to excel at it.

The conclusion is clear. Partnerships work well in adaptive, energetic, positive cultures. They don't do well in reactive, controlling, fearful environments. The connection is equally clear. The factors that we find characteristic of the BHAMs are interactive. They are not a static system of disconnected components. Rather, effective management of the human assets of a company draws on values, strategy, and culture to support partnerships and stimulate widespread communication and risk taking.

Allying With Outsiders

Internal departments create partnerships with external entities as well as with other departments. These can encompass vendors and/or community groups of any kind. Such partnerships may tackle ambitious programs aimed at ameliorating a community problem or even a regional problem. They don't always work. The

Rosemont, Inc., case is an example of a multicompany alliance that did pay off.

Rosemont is a precision instrument manufacturer in the process control industry. It is headquartered in Eden Prairie, Minnesota, just outside Minneapolis. In the mid-1980s, Rosemont's tracking system detected a rapid rise in the cost of health care. As one of a variety of remedies it attempted, Rosemont joined a local alliance called Minnesota's Business Health Care Action Group (BHCAG), a group composed of twenty-two companies, including such well-known partners as Honeywell, 3M, Northern States Power, and Ceridian.

The objective of the partnership was to apply business and quality improvement principles to health care delivery. BHCAG takes a long-term view and requires that all partners commit themselves to the group for a minimum of three years. It strives to improve the quality of health care provided to member company employees and to control the cost of that care. In addition, BHCAG attempts to influence the reform of the regional health care market for the benefit of all citizens. Its long-term approach partners the member companies with providers, carriers, and company employees to collectively improve service.

Members collect and pool data on their health care experiences. Through a number of committees the group is able to bargain for better rates with local providers, assist each other in finding ways to improve administrative functions, and conduct consumer education and communication programs. A telephone help line and group-managed satisfaction surveys provide data on usage and problems. The short-term value of the program was a reduction of health insurance premiums. Rosemont's health care cost per covered employee was 38 percent below the electronic industry mean for the two most recent years surveyed. Overall benefit costs as a percentage of revenue were 22 percent below the industry mean.

The Downside of Partnerships and Alliances

Managing a partnership or an alliance is not always a joy. Because each party has its own agenda and reason for belonging, there are sometimes conflicts. Partnering is a balancing act between competitive and cooperative agendas.

All partners may not have the same level of interest in or commitment to the issues around which the partnership was formed. They have inherently different time frames. Big-company allies can drive small companies crazy over what the smaller firms perceive as their unnecessary conservatism, ambivalence, or delays. On the other hand, some companies choose to form an alliance just to test the water while their associates may be making a wholesale commitment. It's like the story of the chicken and the pig partnership to create a ham and eggs breakfast. For the chicken, it's a natural activity that leaves it no worse for wear. For the pig, it's a total and final commitment. My observation is that often partners are not on the same page. Alliances are even less committed to a single goal. Therefore, when entering into a partnership or alliance of any sort, be prepared for a degree of frustration.

THE HEALTH EXCELLENCE STEERING TEAM

Like Rosemont and thousands of other organizations, Texas Instruments was experiencing runaway health care costs in the mid-1980s. With over 50,000 employees scattered across the United States and in thirty countries, the Dallas-based electronics giant was facing a serious drain on earnings from providing employee health benefits. At the rate benefit costs were rising between 1986 and 1988 the anticipated hit on earnings was projected at $191 million in 1993. Through a variety of internal and external partnerships, the company was able to save nearly 50 percent of projected annual costs, or $63 million, in 1993. This represented a 9 percent contribution to profit.

The base of the internal partnering was the Health Excellence Steering Team. Its membership was made up of a partnership of senior executives and line managers. They worked with employees to prepare a strategy for integrating and transforming health care services into a seamless operation. Collectively, they closed service gaps, identified and removed overlaps, reallocated redundant resources, and defined a set of common metrics for monitoring performance.

The internal network paralleled an external partnership that TI had developed with hospitals, physicians, laboratories, and pharmacies. Rates were negotiated, and over three years the health care network gradually grew. Benefit plans were designed, a performance measurement system developed, and a strategic path was laid out. A supplier quality program was organized with the supplier partners. That helped to identify problems and bottlenecks and to streamline the service. Over the next year employee wait time and abandoned calls both improved by over 50 percent. In addition, the scores on the employee attitude survey showed a marked improvement. In conclusion, TI could identify and quantify the benefit of a long-term approach to building partnerships with all parties involved from the provider to the ultimate customer, the employee. It certainly wasn't a walk in the park, but then few partnerships ever are.

> **Note:** *A critical point about internal partnerships must be made. Many staff departments claim they don't have time for frequent contact with their internal customers. They are too buried in daily transactions to do more than respond when the customer rings their bell. This is one of the main reasons, our surveys revealed, for dissatisfaction with staff work. Specifically, human resources, information services, accounting, and other functions were often described as "bureaucratic, unresponsive, costly, and not adding value." Staff groups must understand that they are now competing with outside vendors who claim that they do have the time to talk with their customers while still providing the service at a competitive price.*

> **BHAM Lesson:** *Effective partnerships require that all members keep their competitive instincts in check and commit themselves to a common goal or run the risk of weakening and undermining the partnership.*

The Best Kind of Partnering: Getting Together With the Customer

Edward Marshall claims that one of the most effective partnerships a company can make is with its key customers.[8] If the company and the customer can be strategically aligned there will be a total focus on customer requirements. You will know their business, product and service needs, and the advantages you can offer them.

He states that this is the basis for what he calls a full-value contract. This is a document that spells out how the two companies are going to work together. It provides a platform for ongoing discussion. Measures are put in place to assess responsiveness. The value to the supplier is that it has a base for planning, communicating, and problem solving.

Treacy and Wiersema offered customer intimacy as one of three possible market disciplines. For the companies that choose this path it is obvious that a deep partnership must be established.[9] Customer-intimate companies deepen and broaden their client support to strengthen the partnership. Their first business access allows them to observe how they and the customer can work effectively. If they are perceptive, future contact continues to open up new avenues of expanded service. This makes the partnership not only useful today but more valuable every day that it exists.

At the Saratoga Institute we learned through repeated surveys and informal discussions with our clients that intimacy was important to them. They like us best when we are face to face with them, and it isn't because of our sparkling personality. People want and need that type of contact, the personal support in what is often a rather confusing world. Our most valued services were those that we provide directly rather than through hard copy products, even though the cost of direct services is much higher. We have found over the past decade that our retention rate with clients is highest when we are able to be in personal contact through training, consultation, or attendance at our national conference.

The principles behind partnering are very similar to those of general benchmarking. After all, benchmarking projects are short-term partnerships. All parties contribute to collective learning. Figure 6-3 lists the key questions to be asked and answered when establishing a partnership at any level. Note that if we can't describe the essence of the issue in a few words, we probably don't fully understand it. We have to cut through the symptom to the competitive issue.

Summary

The trend toward partnering is relatively recent. From the earliest days of the colonists through the 1980s, the people of the United

Figure 6-3. Partnering checklist.

1. Can we succinctly describe the *essential, core* business problem or opportunity that we are considering? _____ Yes   _____ No
   If yes, describe it in ten words or less.*

2. Can this problem be traced to one of the following categories? Check one or more. _____ Productivity _____ Quality _____ Service
   Describe the specific current deficiency by stating it in quantitative and qualitative terms.

3. How will this affect our plans to achieve our corporate strategic imperatives and gain or protect our competitive advantage?
   Describe the link between the productivity, quality, or service issue and our strategic goals.

4. Can we estimate the potential gain or loss from this issue?
   _____ Yes _____ No
   If yes, describe it in product, service, and employee metrics and the earnings impact.

5. Is the source of the problem or opportunity known at this time?
   Describe what is happening or what we would like to have happen.

6. Which functions within our company are or should be involved in the problem or opportunity?
   List general partners who will be directly involved and drive the process and limited partners who may be called on for support activities.

7. What is the projected resource commitment from each partner's function: people, time, capital, equipment, material, information, facilities?

8. Who—from outside, if necessary—can be called on to supply relevant information regarding this issue?
   List by function and location.

---

*There is an inverse correlation between the number of words used in a statement and the amount of truth in the statement.

States were noted for their individualist attitudes. We didn't ask for much help. The Yankee was a supremely self-confident, self-reliant person. Then, around the turn of the century, we began to see the problems that an unfettered individual could cause when he commanded an industrial organization. A series of well-publicized scandals, from Tea Pot Dome in the 1920s through the savings and loan debacle of the 1980s, opened our eyes to the cold truth of the marketplace. The lack of foresight in American executives from the 1960s onward eroded our world market share and shook our self-confidence. This was capped by the greed of the corporate raiders. The good life of the 1950s faded into the layoffs of the late 1980s and 1990s. Resources became scarce. But now, we are beginning to turn around. Our failed self-reliance has given way to cooperation.

Teams, partnerships, and alliances are somewhat different. In some cases, it may only be a semantic distinction. Nevertheless, I see the differences in collaboration as degrees of commitment and degrees of complexity of the problem. My experience is that partners are much more in the game than are teammates. Partners usually seem to feel a greater personal stake in the outcome. This could be because of the nature of the problem. Whatever you name it, it is a collective commitment to an important goal. Partnering clearly is a new trend and an effective way to take on the big challenges.

Common sense suggests that internal partnering is more effective, in most cases, than internal bickering. Energy that used to go into beating out the people across the hall is better used to solve problems. Partnerships generate several benefits beyond the results of the project or program. When people across functions get together they naturally learn about each other and come to appreciate the other's point of view. They have a chance to learn and grow together. Their horizons open up and they become more effective and once again more self-confident.

It must be noted that partnerships take a lot of work, sensitivity, and patience. Whether the functional partnership is internal or external, we must recognize that all partners do not have the same level of interest in or commitment to the project. They also have different internal priorities and different time frames. Successful partnering requires learning new skills of dialogue and a collective commitment to the partnership.

Companies that have challenging, bet-your-company goals need adaptive cultures. These are cultures marked by a spirit of cooperation, enthusiasm, an open mind, and a can-do attitude. This is also the seed bed for partnering. Culture, partnering, and high achievement go together. The finest partnership a company can have is with its customers. Being intimately involved with one's customers is the best insurance a company can have.

All cases point back to Bohm's discussion of dialogue. Partnering has tremendous potential if we can learn how to communicate with our customers. It's more complicated than we think it is. It also has much more potential value than we can imagine. The BHAM cases covered in this chapter, whether they be internal or external examples, relate typical experiences of successful partnerships in which the contact is close and frequent.

References

1. Regis McKenna, *Relationship Marketing* (Reading, Mass.: Addison-Wesley, 1991).
2. Lewis Carroll, *Through the Looking Glass*, Chap. 6.
3. Peter Senge, *The Fifth Discipline* (New York: Doubleday, 1990), chap. 3, pp. 239–249.
4. Ibid.
5. Ralph H. Kilmann, M. J. Saxton, and Roy Serpa (eds.), *Gaining Control of the Corporate Culture* (San Francisco: Jossey-Bass, 1986), p. 356.
6. John P. Kotter, *The Leadership Factor* (New York: The Free Press, 1988).
7. Nicholas Imparato and Oren Harari, *Jumping the Curve* (San Francisco: Jossey-Bass, 1994), p. 190.
8. Edward M. Marshall, *Transforming the Way We Work* (New York: AMACOM, 1995).
9. Michael Treacy and Fred Wiersema, *The Discipline of Market Leaders* (Reading, Mass.: Addison-Wesley, 1995), pp. 133–135.

7

Collaboration

How the Best Support Each Other Internally, Share Resources and Competencies, and Outperform the Competition

Collaboration is a form of collective support that goes beyond mere cooperation. Collaboration describes a form of partnering that is centered within a function. Like many interactions, it is often so pervasive as to go unnoticed. It's "just the way we are" or "just the way we do things here." You see it when one department or section within a function shares its idea or plan with other departments or sections within that function. The purpose is to see what effect the plan will have on other groups.

For example, when the compensation group is planning on changing the structure of the pay plan, in most companies compensation simply gets the approval of the CEO and senior line executives and then tells the recruiters, trainers, and employee relations people what is coming. In a collaborative environment the compensation group reverses this process. It sets up an informal team to review the issues involved in a different pay plan. Questions fly about the room regarding the need for a new structure, the effects it will have on recruitment, how employees might view it, and what the trainers must do with their supervisory and management courses to teach the new plan. In the best cases, representatives of middle management and first-line supervisors are also brought into the discussion as well. You might think this is the norm if you hadn't experienced the self-centered life-style of many organizations.

Collaboration is not solely the province of the human resources function. It works the same way in any group. Marketing might involve advertising, public and investor relations, sales administration, and sales in a discussion of a new marketing program. Within the finance arena, the controller might call in accounts receivable, payables, cost accounting, and even treasury to critique an idea. The point is the same as in partnering. By calling on others who have a stake in something, you get the benefit of their ideas and resources, which help you to bring out a better plan or product and accomplish it more quickly. Probably the greatest value of collaboration lies in the insights that others bring to your function.

Just as partnering is an outgrowth of a cultural value, so is collaboration. It is a living example of the corporate values. Collaboration is more an ethic than a system. It is difficult to separate it from partnering. Collaboration does not preclude partnering. In many ways it is just a change of venue. Whereas partnering is across functions, collaboration is within a function. The idea is that we do better work in one department when we involve others. In the case of collaboration, the others are primarily those within one's own function. That's what makes it a little different from normal partnering. The difference may be subtle or even indistinct at times. However, we found that collaboration was not a common practice in The Rest the way it was in the BHAMs. My experience of nearly forty years in business is that departments don't cooperate well within their own functional borders. There is often jealousy and turf protection just as there is between functions.

In large, impersonal organizations, people can become so focused on their own particular responsibilities that they forget the interactive aspects of their own department, to say nothing of what's going on across functions. They think of themselves as being residents of that little box on the organization chart. A chart, while useful as a corporate map, can be deceptive because charts, like maps, are fixed and static.

Organizations are anything but static. Their dynamism is

breathtaking. The lines that connect functions, like the lines that connect cities on a map, suggest that there is a prescribed and best way to go from point A to point B. Of course, the best way really depends on what you value—speed or beautiful scenery. In a company there are many lines of communication and interaction, most of them invisible and underground. Similar to telecommunications, many channels of communication are buried or exist as invisible signals flowing from one satellite or relay station to another. We all know the power of the grapevine and of the informal organization. Many key decisions come out of informal discussions around the water cooler or over lunch. The organization chart does not take this into consideration.

A company that practices collaboration and partnering is doing just what top management usually says it wants: working as a team. Teamwork is the rallying cry today. More and more people tell us that their company is notable for its team orientation. The major inconsistency is that management is still rewarding individual performance while calling for teamwork.

John Kotter talks about companies in which partnering and collaboration are markedly absent. In describing nonadaptive cultures he points out that what people most often say they care about is "themselves."[1] The norm in these companies is to behave in a closed, cautious manner. They are highly political places where the key value is guarded communication leading to self-protection. This is not where you find the benefits of collaboration.

LEADERSHIP BUILDS COLLABORATION

In early 1989, Priscilla Smith took over direction of the human resources function at Prudential Property and Casualty. She was committed to, and personally prepared to, launching a new strategy for the function as a value-adding operation. In this she had the full support of the division president. However, when she introduced the concept, her management team objected. Members claimed that with several other changes coursing through the organization, this would not be a good time for another. She listened to their concerns and decided it would be wiser to wait a while. But she wasn't to be put off. Three months later, she began the program of repositioning the department.

The key point in this case is how she turned a loose-knit group of personnel administrators into a powerful value-adding team.

In retrospect, it was a clear case of committed leadership. Smith started by creating an environment of openness and trust. She encouraged communication and participation. She modeled this behavior by frequently holding both formal and informal meetings with all staff members to communicate company news. With the full department team assembled she would tell them what was going on in the company in various areas. She encouraged them to stretch and to become involved in issues beyond their prescribed duties. Then she and others told stories of how someone in the department had added value to an internal customer. Each week several stories were told describing both successes and failures. Smith made it a point to own up to her failures, thereby demonstrating that it was okay to risk and fail so long as one learned from it. This began the process of opening up and cross-communicating between sections.

When talking to her management team, Smith told it, "Push back hard on me. Tell me what I am missing." She generated an atmosphere of constructive challenging. They borrowed worksheets from the quality program to analyze their improvement efforts. The forms required input from everyone. This helped develop a natural practice of not moving forward in an isolated fashion. One major project typified the collaborative style that was developing.

There came a time when it was necessary to modify some parts of the performance management system. This was launched in the claims division, the largest group in the company. The process started with a partnering approach utilizing the knowledge and experience of claims division supervisors and managers. One of the principal needs was to find a better process to resolve performance deficiencies. Two goals were established. One was to reduce their time spent on the process. The other was to reduce the amount of work required by the supervisor. The existing process required the supervisor to do all the work of planning each employee's performance improvement. Now, management wanted to shift accountability for improvement to the individual employee. The training function and field human resource units were charged with designing communications and training materials that would support the changed behavior. The staff and line managers worked together to determine what was feasible. Then they tested their ideas with other managers and supervisors and the customers. After passing their inspection, they took the plan for the new procedure to the executive level for final approval.

The biggest change in the procedure was to have every associate develop his or her own improvement plan. This could work only if there was some support from training or the employees' supervisors. Many lower-level employees couldn't do this by themselves. They had never before been asked to think on their own about their careers or their performance. A key feature of the new approach was to give employees who had to work out a personal improvement program a day off with pay to sit down and think out what they had to do differently and how they could make that work for them. They were to be charged with coming back to their supervisor the next day with an answer as to how or whether their plan would work.

The division managers and supervisors welcomed this shift of responsibility, even though it involved a cost. However, the day was won when Priscilla pointed out to them that the cost of one day's pay is nothing compared to an employee's continued marginal performance or termination. With turnover costing upwards of six months' pay per person it was a good gamble. The strange part was that this idea was a major stumbling block for the top executive group. However, when the managers demonstrated the amount of time they would be saving—time that could be allocated to value-adding activity—the executives caved in.

The executives' initial resistance to the new procedure is an example of the lack of respect that top management has for the rank and file. When confronted with proposals like this, their reaction is often that the employee will take advantage of the company. By contrast, in BHAM companies, the senior management group thinks positively about people, and because it demonstrates a positive outlook, an atmosphere of mutual trust and respect spreads to the rest of the organization. BHAM companies try to have people understand that their purpose goes beyond the activity that consumes their day. Management puts together many projects and programs like the one just described to help people see how they are connected to the larger purposes of the company. From this comes motivation, lower turnover, and better performance.

In looking back, it is clear that partnering and collaborative teaming were the keys to success at Prudential's P&C group. That is what distinguished it from the larger corporation and from other groups within Pru. Everyone in human resources in P&C was involved at one point or another. They challenged the boss but kept the process moving ahead efficiently. There was some concern that while the hardheaded claims personnel at headquarters could handle the strain of such decision making, in the field it might be a different story. Therefore, the program had to be introduced differently in the two venues. Teaming up training with field management brought out a skill-building class to help employees work on their personal improvement programs. Field personnel received ongoing support in the form of communications and training and were able to incorporate this change.

All staff had to learn to play the new game. This meant that consulting skills had to be instilled in both the professional staff and the supporting associates. This was somewhat risky. On the other hand, how could you have professionals who saw their role as value-adding consultants and an administrative staff who thought they were there only to handle transactions? The efforts of the professionals would be diminished, if not unknowingly sabotaged, by the support staff. Training both professionals and staff support together reinforced the collaborative ethic vertically as well as horizontally and turned it into a powerful bonding exercise because it broke down the walls between the two groups.

The new skills developed at PruPac paid off in a big way. The PruPac human resources group had the highest overall performance of more than 500 similar departments as reported in our 1993 benchmark survey.[2] In concrete terms, this means that across all aspects of human asset management, PruPac's costs, time cycles, and productivity levels were in the top 5 percent. Priscilla's skills didn't go unnoticed. When the P&C group underwent a major restructuring, Priscilla was given a job in marketing. At the time this book was going to press, Priscilla was moving back into the P&C group as vice president, Product Planning.

One Size Does Not Fit All

Human interaction seldom fits well into simple formulas. People working together exhibit a wide range of psychological, emotional, and physical idiosyncrasies. It's not as simple as statistical process control in which the process is quite visible and unbiased and the system formulaic. That's what makes working with people so interesting as well as vexing.

In every BHAM company we studied we found collaboration practiced in a slightly different manner and in varying degrees. That's why it cannot be pictured in a simple diagram or described in a simple prescription. The closest I can come to expressing the idea is shown in Figure 7-1. Here you see, in a typical or traditional organization, limited communication between a department plan (compensation) and other groups. There is little involvement with anyone other than senior management, which has to bless the plan. By contrast, in the BHAM organization, many people are consulted. In the end they all feel they have had their say. The central proposition is: We value sharing our ideas and plans with other interested parties who have some value to add or who may be affected by our actions.

Figure 7-1. Contrasting lines of communication as typical and BHAM staff operations.

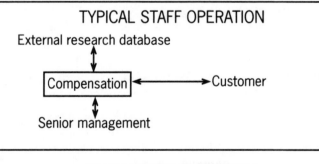

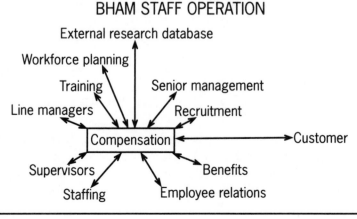

THE GOOD SAMARITAN

In 1991, three primary care hospitals, a home health care agency, and a medical foundation in Silicon Valley (San Jose area of California) merged under the name of the Good Samaritan Health System. Good Sam employs approximately 4,500 people.

The objective of the merger was to improve regional health care while reducing its cost to the community. The merger faced all the interorganizational problems you might expect. To facilitate the changes several methods and programs were instituted:

❑ TQM philosophy
❑ Employee communications
❑ Business planning training
❑ Managerial and employee development
❑ Employee assistance programs (EAP)
❑ Ongoing measurement and evaluation

The internal objectives were to speed the changeover with a minimum of disruption. Throughout the next two years many functions got together in partnerships. Within functions the staffs worked under a collaborative ethic to make it happen. At the end, they had pulled it off and were able to keep the turnover rate of key-skill personnel 30 percent below the health care industry average.

The following are abbreviated examples of which functions were involved and how they interacted.

❑ *EAP—Employee relations and training.* EAP's counseling services kept track of their contact trends and identified problems with which employee relations and training could help. By working together to provide training and support in focused areas they were able to retain employees needed in the merged organization.

❑ *CEO—Training.* The CEO, working with the training department, developed a business planning course for managers. The CEO personally conducts the course. He links it with Good Sam's Mission-and-Vision Plan as well as with the five-year strategic plan.

❑ *CEO/VPs—HR—Internal communications.* The CEO and the division vice presidents regularly conduct "cracker-barrel" meetings with employees throughout the company. These are informal discussions featuring questions and answers as well as opinions and suggestions from the bottom up. This program is augmented by a President's Hotline using a voice-mail system. The president also responds directly to questions by publishing the issues and answers in the employee newsletter every two weeks.

❑ *Data and measurement systems.* All parties with a stake in the data sharing and performance measurement got together to develop a uniform system. The goal was to save time and effort and ensure data integrity.

Through these efforts the leaders of the company were able to weld together five different entities into a cohesive whole. They didn't do it perfectly, but they completed the journey with fewer casualties and less disruption than is normal when different cultures and structures merge.

Failure and Success: The Reasons

Gary Hamel and C. K. Prahalad have identified two generic reasons for failure among great companies. One is the inability of the company to escape its past; the other is its inability to invest in its future.[3] In both types of cases, the human element is the defining feature. All the companies studied had performed exceptionally well for decades. Yet eventually they fell because they became complacent in several ways. Success bred arrogance and arrogance led to ruin. The most telling factors revolved around management's belief that structure and resources would carry the day. These were command-and-control structures and capital resources, not human resources. The giants knew they could invest in structural layers and outspend the competition. But the upstart competition believed that human intellectual capital working with efficient processes would conquer cash any day. In the end, the upstarts proved their hypothesis.

Two Process Successes

An example of how process focus succeeds is provided by Hewlett-Packard. Early in the 1990s a few top executives at H-P became concerned that they might fall behind the curve in applications of digital technology. CEO Lewis Platt came up with the equation $HP = MC2$, where M stands for measurement and the two Cs stand for computing and communications. Using partnering and collaborative methods, he led managers in bringing together people from different sections, departments, and functions to identify new multibillion-dollar opportunities that would "turn markets upside down." Each succeeding project cut across traditionally defined business unit borders. To date, the partnering has created several new product lines that are on the leading edge of the market. By substituting a commitment to cross-sector communications for the traditional structures and processes, the company reaped the benefits of reinvention and leadership.

EDS provides another example of a cross-functional process working. When General Motors bought Electronic Data Systems in 1984, GMC turned over its worldwide computer and telecommunications operations to EDS. Ten years later, EDS had more than 70,000 employees in thirty-one countries. About that time, CEO Les Alberthal became concerned about motivating the world's largest data network company. In the course of providing managers with the insights, knowledge, and tools they would need to reinvent EDS for the twenty-first century, a small group of middle managers set themselves up as the "corporate change team." Without an official charter, they brought their viewpoints and skills from different sections into a collaborative effort focused on rethinking corporate directions. Realizing quickly that they could not pull off such an enormous challenge, they lobbied the company's leadership council to support the effort. In short, they got the attention and resources they needed to lead a change in the strategic architecture of the company. The lesson is that whether you are in a 4,000-person company in one community or a megacorporation boasting worldwide operations, the principles of partnering and collaboration apply.

> **BHAM Lesson:** *If we succeed there is glory enough for everyone. If we fail there will be no heroes.*

Process Competence

Boxes on organization charts no longer mean anything. Through the 1970s the command-and-control mentality ruled. If the line of communication ran from your box to another box that was the protocol you followed. Today, with network technology and a more egalitarian social ethic in place, anyone can communicate with anyone. In fact, many organizations encourage cross-functional communications. This difference can be likened to the difference between a telephone system and a two-way radio broadcasting site. The organization chart shows us where the telephone lines are strung and requires that communications operate in a sequential mode—one sender to one receiver (not counting teleconferencing). In today's practice, many workers now have a two-way radio site from which they can broadcast in all directions simultaneously. It's called a computer network, e.g., e-mail and the worldwide Internet. In this case, effective communications depend on the competence of the players and the effective application of the process capability more than on the structure of who reports to whom and who is where on the chart.

Collaborative organizations use process competence to share resources and personal competencies. David Ulrich at the University of Michigan has lectured extensively on reframing the age-old question of centralization versus decentralization.[4] He tells us that we need a new question that has nothing to do with structure. That is a turf battle for which we have no time. Figure 7-2 shows that the

Figure 7-2. Power/control vs. service/value issues.

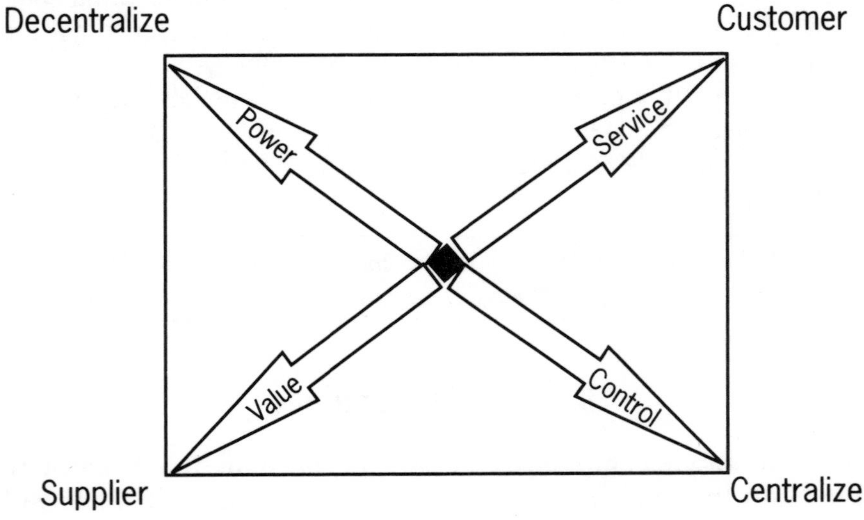

Decentralize .... Customer

Power   Service

Value   Control

Supplier .... Centralize

traditional structure battle deals with functional power bases. The service/value focus deals with teaming to serve customer needs, thereby obtaining value for the company. The energy has to go into integration, process, and teamwork. The focus is the customer. The process is resource and competence sharing—not competing.

A model of this rationale in operation is the trend in larger organizations to set up what are labeled shared service centers. The idea is that any staff function or part of it can be placed in an integrative service center. This means that specialized, expert, staff resources and competencies not directly in contact with the customer are centralized for efficiency. Typically, the shared service center houses some hiring activities, compensation and benefits administration, parts of training, and some employee relations services such as employee assistance programs (EAP). The theory is that the line is now free to focus its resources on the customer. When the line user needs a specialized service, he goes first to the shared service center. If the center can't support the request, then the user is free to seek the service elsewhere. The end game is that if the shared service function does the job, it stays in business. If it doesn't, the function is usually outsourced or in a few cases delegated back to the line. The rationale for this is twofold: (1) It makes the staff functions more efficient, responsive, and collaborative; (2) it keeps the line resources fixed on the customer.

Collaboration Checklist

Because collaboration is a form of partnering, the same types of questions are used as criteria for identifying the affected parties who should be involved. The issues are quite similar to those that arise with partnering in that working together is a generic art form simply applied in different settings. One of the key differences with collaboration is that the problem or opportunity is often on a smaller scale than what stems from interorganizational issues. See Figure 7-3 for a suggested list of questions for setting up a collaborative project.

Summary

Collaboration and partnering are almost identical in process terms. They both involve working with people outside one's own section

Figure 7-3. Collaborative partnering checklist.

1. What is the *business problem* or *opportunity* we are considering?
   Describe in ten words or less how it is adversely affecting our customers.

2. Can the problem be traced to one of the following categories: productivity,
   quality, or service?
   Describe the current deficiency by stating it in quantitative terms.

3. How does/will it affect our requirement to support the company's key strategic imperatives?
   Describe the link between the productivity, quality, or service issue and our
   corporate strategic goals.

4. What is the potential gain or loss in product, service, or employee factors
   and in cash?

5. Is the source of the problem or opportunity known at this time?
   Describe where it exists.

6. Which functions within our company are or should be involved in solving
   the problem or exploiting the opportunity?

7. What is the projected resource commitment from each function in terms of
   people, time, equipment, material, information, and facilities?

8. How do we sell them on committing resources to this case?

---

or department. The principal difference is that collaboration is
most often seen within a function. That is, several departments
such as recruiting, training, and compensation might be working
collectively on the implications and design of a pay plan restructuring.

Often collaborative actions are nearly invisible. They are such
a basic part of a BHAM set that one stops looking at them. They
are an ethic. They become part of the function or corporate culture.
The principal value that collaboration generates, beyond more effective solutions to problems, is that it breaks down barriers and
misunderstandings between disciplines within a function. It also

brings together staff and professional personnel in a more harmonious and egalitarian system. It stimulates teamwork and sets the stage for more effective action in the future.

Collaboration is an excellent example of how BHAMs turn to people rather than to things to solve problems. The focus here is on process rather than structure. The *how* of problem solving or management is always more important and sometimes more difficult than the *what*. Human intellectual capital is more effective than cash in building organizations that will prosper in the long term. The collaborators marshal resources and competence and apply them to process opportunities. The result is a vibrant, positive organization in which everyone is heard and feels they are contributing.

References

1. John P. Kotter, *The Leadership Factor* (New York: The Free Press, 1988), p. 50.
2. *Best in America Guidebook* (Saratoga, Calif.: Saratoga Institute, 1993).
3. Gary Hamel and C. K. Prahalad, *Competing for the Future* (Boston: Harvard Business School Press, 1994), pp. 111–120.
4. David Ulrich, conversations and unpublished lectures on process versus structure.

8

Innovation and Risk

*How the Best Manage Risk
and Innovate to
Speed-Learning and Time-to-Market*

The director of human resources opened the door and I followed him into the meeting room. He smiled warmly as only an Irishman can and greeted everyone. Then he dropped the bomb. His words went something like this: "Effective immediately, this department is closed. I'm sorry, but we are all out of a job."

After a short pause to let everyone take back the breath that had just been knocked out of them, he continued:

> Top management has decided that there needs to be a change in the approach to managing the human assets of this company. From here on, human resources services are going to be delivered in a new way. A company is being formed to do that. It is called HR Incorporated. You are welcome to apply for a job. Personally speaking, I hope you do. I would enjoy continuing to work with you. If you want to apply, there are job descriptions and application forms on the table in back. I will start holding interviews tomorrow. Oh, by the way, I am the new president of HR Inc. If you have any questions, I will be in my office. Good luck.

In a few minutes some of the people headed for the back table. As they rummaged through the job descriptions in search of positions comparable to the ones they had held until ten minutes earlier, they became confused. None of the standard human resources management titles were offered. No recruiting jobs, no compensation specialists, no benefits administrators or managers. Instead they found job listings for production, sales, service, distribution, administration, and the like. As the director had said, it was a company.

To make a long story short, after a period of milling about and holding muffled conversations, a confused and somewhat upset group descended on the office of the former vice president of human resources, now the president of HR Inc. After briefly discussing the basic reasons for the sudden change, he explained what was happening.

Until now his attempts at driving change in the department, which he had inherited just a couple of months earlier, had met with stiff resistance. Many of the specialists and managers had been in the same job for years and had reached a point of simple Pavlovian reaction to calls for services. As the company began a new period of spirited growth, the old HR department was found to be ineffective. Still, staff members wouldn't change their habits. Finally, using a well-crafted plan, the director decided to stun everyone enough to get their attention. Facing corporate execution, they finally listened.

Several were angry. A few of the younger, less entrenched people were quite happy. The risk had been that not only might several key people quit and leave him short-handed for a while but, worse yet, they might head for the CEO's office and draw on long-standing personal relationships to lobby for his head. As it turned out, a couple tried this move but were rebuffed by the CEO (who had been in on the plan, of course). One person tried her version of the silent treatment, but when colleagues came to empty her desk for her, she woke up quickly and decided to apply.

Over the next six months the department was restructured and a new spirit emerged. The risk had been managed and the innovative approach to reorganizing launched a much more effective operation.

The Father of Innovation

If necessity is the mother of invention, then risk is the father of innovation. Nothing new happens unless someone risks abandoning the old way of doing things. Risk is an inherent characteristic of business. No company is above having to take risks. The successful companies are good risk managers as well as innovators. In the current market and as far ahead as we can see, companies will be faced with constant, rapid, all-encompassing change. Some pundits believe that we will be well into the second decade of the twenty-first century before we complete the transformation from an industrial to an information society.

Personally, I believe that we will not see a settling in until some time after that. The reason is the unceasing, high-speed changes that are being offered, indeed driven, by technology. These affect not only electronics but also medicine, biology, genetics, aerospace, transportation, and numerous other areas.

As one example, we have just begun to touch the surface of information technology. With voice recognition, the keyboard will become obsolete. Anyone who isn't speech-impaired will find voice technology becoming increasingly user-friendly. Worldwide, nearly instantaneous communication will drive markets at a frantic pace. Already, you can push a bank card into an ATM in most major cities and in less than thirty seconds draw funds from your account 10,000 miles away. You can order a present for a friend from an airplane and have it delivered within a couple of days—a handy service for forgetful spouses.

All these will seem like amusing toys to the historians of the latter half of the twenty-first century. Just as the telegraph and the locomotive revolutionized communications and transportation and opened the American West to physical exploitation and development in the second half of the nineteenth century, so the marvels of electronic technology will aid in developing human capabilities in the next millennium.

As the technology gives us capability, it simultaneously charges a price in terms of responsiveness. In 1804, when Lewis and Clark set out from St. Louis to explore the territory of the Louisiana Purchase, it took six weeks for information to travel from the Mississippi River region to Washington, D.C. No one expected responsiveness. It wasn't even imaginable. Today, it is demanded if we want to stay in the game. Markets that used to occupy buildings are now virtual. That is, they exist simultaneously worldwide. And they change continually. In such an environment it must be permissible for people to take risks and make mistakes. If we try to exert too much control, we stifle activity and certainly curtail creativity. We all make mistakes when we try new things. If we learn, we grow. But we cannot be competitive without risk.

RISK MANAGING DURING A DOWNSIZING

Charleston Area Medical Center serves the greater Charleston, West Virginia, area with three hospitals staffed by nearly 5,000 employees. Each campus has a specialty, and they are all tied together under one medical center corporation. Early in the 1990s, CAMC was forced into a downsizing.

The center's Employee Relations Committee is charged with supporting employee morale and being the voice of the people. The committee is made up of fifty nonmanagement personnel who serve overlapping terms. They have access to all employee programs during the design phase. This can be risky in that committee members are free to discuss developments with employees from their departments.

The ER Committee members realized that one objective of the reduction in force was to cut operating expenses. They also felt it was time for an employee attitude survey. Now every professional knows that you don't do an attitude survey during or shortly after a downswing, for obvious reasons. Nevertheless, after due deliberation, the committee decided that it could carry out the survey successfully under just such conditions. Furthermore, it would do it without the expensive assistance of a local consultant. This risk was exacerbated by the fact that the committee was composed of personnel from outside the human resources department. No one on the committee had the professional credentials usually required for this type of work. In spite of this, in a tour de force of salesmanship, they convinced management to take the risk of letting them do the job themselves. Considering that this group of amateurs could have wreaked havoc during a very sensitive period, one wonders why management decided to trust the committee and take the risk. Its faith is one of the reasons CAMC is a BHAM company. Management believes in its people.

Knowing that they were pretty green in this arena, committee members decided to restrict their survey to six direct and simple questions. They eschewed all jargon in their questions. As one example, they asked employees, "What bugs you about CAMC?" This is a highly negative way of presenting the question. It almost begs for a complaint. Nevertheless, the surveys were distributed to a random sample of employees. Typically, a 45 percent response rate to surveys is considered good. The committee's survey response rate was a phenomenal 96.7 percent! In thirty years of working around surveys, I never saw that high a response. The committee undertook to read every one of the 600 completed surveys and then conducted its own nonscientific analysis and follow-up. Here are a few of the programs that resulted.

❑ *An employee newsletter.* Employees said they felt they received more information via the grapevine than through formal channels. So, the committee started a newsletter called *Grapevine.* It contains information on CAMC's business and employee issues. Employees can ask questions and make inputs to the newsletter.

❑ *Videotaping of department meetings.* Because the hospital operates on a three-shift, twenty-four-hour, seven-day-week schedule, many employees are unable to attend meetings. The videos keep them informed.

❑ *Self-directed work teams.* Employees felt that work wasn't getting done as efficiently as it might be. They were allowed to organize self-directed teams to do budgeting and hiring and to make many production decisions.

❑ *Presentation skills.* Employees believed that many managers needed training on how to conduct effective meetings and make presentations. Top management was persuaded to provide the training.

This is just one recent and rather dramatic example of risk management at CAMC. Risk is a central part of the company's management ethos. CAMC was one of the earliest to go self-insured on health care. Success in that program led to self-insuring disability programs as well. These were followed by a flexible benefit plan. Today none of this would be big news. But in the mid-1970s it was a leap into the unknown.

Management involves employees in many self-educating ventures. They equip employees at relatively low levels with flip charts and materials to explain to their peers how certain programs work. The employees take this responsibility seriously. They study before they present. Management believes that respected peers can convey information and get feedback for the company that others cannot do as well. When employees see one of their own presenting, they open up and express their true feelings. They make useful suggestions that help management to design programs in ways that enable employees to take ownership.

Because many positions in the hospital demand top-level skills, CAMC has a Recruitment and Retention Committee. This is made up of human resources personnel and department representatives. The committee's mission is to develop recruitment and retention strategies. From this has come an exit interview program that yields trend data on employees' reasons for quitting. On the basis of this, CAMC has been able to make changes that led to greater retention of RNs. A tuition reimbursement program also came out of this committee. Collectively, the work of the RRC has contributed to CAMC's having a very competitive turnover rate.

Risk and Trust

Successful risk management is built on trust. Top executives must learn to trust their people. Throughout our research, we found both small and large examples of risk taking that were based on trust. Being in touch with its employees helps management sense how much risk is involved in any given situation. Trust doesn't always help executives sleep well at night. But in the long run, they learn through trials, errors, and successes where the risk level can be set.

At CAMC, risk taking worked because top management knew its people. Contact is the key, but "management by walking around" isn't the answer. That phase is simplistic. Even Tom Peters and Bob Waterman, who popularized it in *In Search of Excellence*, admitted later that this was only a surface manifestation of something more fundamental. However, by then it was too late. The term has entered the management vocabulary, and just like the misinterpretation of Fred Herzberg's "money isn't a motivator" thirty years ago, it is a convenient and appealing platitude. Nevertheless, the idea of getting out of the ivory tower and onto the shop or office floor is valid. The more you are in touch with your people, the more they are likely to learn about you. In the end, you not only realize how capable they are but they understand how much they are expected to risk.

Management's reluctance to allow low-level personnel to manage risk is ironic. The irony of management distrust for those lower down lies in the reality that the lower one is on the economic scale, the more one must risk and learn every day just to survive. When you are living close to the poverty level, you either get very creative or you starve. Some executives need to get off their biases and acknowledge that the people who are actually doing the work may have some pretty good ideas on how to do it better. If they make risk a requirement, and support it when the innovation goes haywire, the people can handle it. When you treat employees like intelligent, worthwhile human beings instead of like zombies, you might discover how wise and trustworthy they can be.

Giving Permission to Fail

Consultant Edward M. Marshall argues for a Risk-Forgiveness Agreement.[1] He claims that to encourage risk we have to forgive mistakes so long as we learn from them in the process. Our folklore is filled with people who risked and failed and risked again. Presidents Lincoln and Truman are well-known examples of eminent people who were business failures earlier in their lives. Chester Carlson, the father of xerography, labored for years, in the process smelling up his wife's kitchen, trying unsuccessfully to uncover the secrets of photocopying. The archetype of all failures was Thomas Edison. He and his research staff tried unsuccessfully 10,000 times before finally getting the right material for the filament for the electric lightbulb. Where there is no forgiveness, there will be no risk.

In today's environment of lean staffs and constant change, taking a risk is often a good way to scar your career. Not only do risk takers have to fight the process technology management is trying to improve, they often have to fight bureaucratic procedures and two-faced supervisors. It is much safer simply to do what one is told and keep one's head down as succeeding rounds of layoffs sweep through the organization like the plague.

The management problem with this attitude is that when it is the cultural norm the company has no chance for market leadership. After all, you can't beat the competition by outspending them if your researchers are afraid to go out on a limb with a crazy idea that might just work. It is popular to talk about creating a learning organization. But how do you learn if people are afraid to apply for a test in which failure invites disaster? If you want innovation, you must not only accept risk and mistakes, you must demand them. Having opened the door, then you must push people into the risk-innovation arenas. These are the public places in the company where people are celebrated for the many great ideas that didn't quite work as well as for the few that did!

RAYNET

Raynet, located in Menlo Park, California, is a fiberoptics subsidiary of Raychem, the $1.6-billion computer systems company. From its launch in 1987, it grew from 80 employees to nearly 1,000 in only 6 years. As the company grew out of its adolescent phase, it found it needed to build systems around such issues as job evaluation and job compensation. Typically, companies are very wary of disclosing job and salary information, and with good reason. Pay and job levels are very personal issues fraught with great emotion. Raynet decided to open the system to all employees.

Under the Raynet system, all employees can gain access to information regarding their jobs and salary grades and salary ranges via electronic mail. As you might imagine, managers were somewhat reluctant to put such volatile data on the internal network, even if it was supposedly secure from outside intruders. Still, openness and trust fit Raynet's philosophy of management, so the system was launched. The objective was twofold: (1) to show employees that management had no reason to be secretive about pay issues, and (2) to reinforce the culture of open communication. In this system, if an employee feels that his job is not properly described, he can bring the question up to his manager, who in turn has it reviewed by the compensation department. If the employee's view turns out to be correct, the job is reclassified and pay adjusted accordingly.

In the beginning, there was a good deal of confusion and many calls to compensation for clarification or umpiring of disputes. However, within less than a year this tapered off. Now, both employees and managers understand the system, and most questions are solved within the department. Employees are especially pleased that there is a fair, accurate, and open method for assessing their jobs and an avenue of appeal if necessary. The payoff has been no abuse of the system, a culture of trust that serves all sides well, and low turnover rates.

Intrapreneuring and Risk Taking

It is impossible to innovate without taking risks. Some companies truly encourage reasonable risks and actually make seed money available for new projects that involve risk. Others talk risk but reward conformity. In the mid-1980s the term *intrapreneuring* was made popular by Gifford Pinchot.[2] Suddenly, as with similar fads, intrapreneuring became the buzzword among consultants and business writers. But not everyone was hopping on the bandwagon. The earliest rumblings of major, invisible change were starting to hit the marketplace. Washington was on a new defense spending spree that was driving up the national debt, and the Japanese were continuing to bite off chunks of many North American markets.

At one end of the continuum, Reagan's supply-side economists were urging investment for growth. Innovation and risk were the bywords. At the other end, the demand-minded were hunkering down and waiting for the cycle to swing in their favor. These latter executives were calling for expense controls, not innovation or intrapreneuring. Quality programs were becoming the rage as a means of reducing break-even points and of recapturing market share. But towards the end of the decade the supply-siders were in rout and the first tidal waves of layoffs rose. *Downsizing* entered the vocabulary. In that environment no one in his right mind wanted to stick his neck out and be an intrapreneur. Even today there are many who haven't forgotten that it is often safer to keep your mouth shut and not attract attention with bold moves that might not pan out.

Consider the range of risks that plagues innovation. The first and most obvious is the failure of the innovation itself. You might have a great idea, Orville, but if you can't make it fly you have only a paper miracle. Second is customer rejection. You might be ahead of the market, as Federal Express was with its fax delivery business. Even if you get to market, but haven't come out with a barrier to competition, the big guys could leapfrog your position overnight. If the domestic or foreign competitors don't take your market away, you might find that you have overextended yourself and can't support your own innovation. (I have to admit that we did this at Saratoga Institute in the early 1990s when we offered a benchmarking network service. It was so popular that we found we couldn't service or support it. We were forced to drop it and it hurt our reputation for the next two years.) Finally, you may have a great product, but an unpredictable event such as an oil embargo or a recession changes the game. Given all these impediments, it is no wonder that many executives would rather follow the innovators than take on the risk of leading.

INNOVATION AT THE MEMORIAL SLOAN-KETTERING CANCER CENTER

MSKCC, as it is usually referred to, is a major cancer treatment center located in New York City and employing over 5,500 people. World-class performance in medical and management sciences is the hallmark of the center. Top management has always supported ideas that showed the possibility of producing improvements. However, one of the requirements for management support is a quantitative analysis of any proposal. This does not always mean a detailed accounting-type analysis of future value. It does mean solid, verifiable, objective data based on some empirical research. This applies to human asset management as well as to medical or administrative matters. The belief is that progress is dependent on marshaling two resources: capital and human skills. One without the other isn't enough. Simply outspending the competition seldom wins the race. Taking nothing away from MSKCC's record of medical achievement, it is in the second resource arena—human skills—that the center has a record of high risk, high gain.

Ed Kleinert was a neurology and oncology researcher who moved to the administrative side of the center in the early 1980s. He carried with him management's belief that administration's mandate was to do more than move paper or electronic data around. First, it was to enrich the working environment. The idea was to free the hands to engage the brain. Second, the mandate was to do it before it was done to you. In other words, lead the race or get trampled by the herd. The corollary is that the race is never finished. If you lead at the end of one lap, that doesn't give you the right to relax and coast if you want to be leading at the end of the next lap.

Because a medical center's success is driven by the skills of its staff, Kleinert decided to focus on improving the way the center attracted and hired its talent. As many as 25,000 to 30,000 job applications and résumés create an annual paper blizzard for the center. These must be processed in, responded to, stored, and retrieved on demand. For the employment function it meant that recruiters had to physically scan every applicant's paper, sometimes several pages long, and make a decision as to its fate. The recruiters were seasoned professionals who spent at least 25 percent of their time reading.

Today, there are automated applicant tracking systems that scan incoming applications and store them according to a given protocol. In 1983 that was not the case. It was a manual job. There was a realization that MSKCC was spending many thousands of dollars annually through advertising and other recruitment programs to build an applicant pool. However, once an application or résumé was received and filed, it was often hard to locate. Imagine trying to find an application that came in four months ago once it entered a manual filing system. At best, it was a mind-bending task; at worst, it failed to produce the desired document. To solve this, using a PC-XT and dBase III, the staff developed a relational database supporting their first automated applicant tracking system.

By early 1984, the system was in service. Performance data were built into the system so that the system's effectiveness and efficiency could be monitored. This point is critical. Performance-level reporting was part of the original program. The next step was obvious and management supported it because the first step had proved its worth. In 1985, the center started developing a local area network to distribute data to recruiting staff. It also automated letters to applicants and standard correspondence along with additional reports on the yields of the system. It continued to migrate to higher levels of automation. Still, after the paper was filed it had to be retrieved from a central data file. This brought about a scanning capability that allowed the applicant data to be converted to electronic files for ease of retrieval. Today, applications can be scanned for key words and matched with one or more positions. Recruiters can call for specific prequalified applications and spend their time interviewing applicants and working with the hiring supervisors.

One would think that the recruiters would have welcomed this innovation. On the contrary, like all of us, initially they preferred the old method. They liked to have their hands on the paper. They complained that a good candidate might be lost because the key words weren't there. They didn't trust the scanner to work. The list of fears and excuses went on and on. However, gradually through usage, even the most recalcitrant of recruiters experienced their added capability.

In real time the recruiter can be talking to the hiring manager and simultaneously send a search query for applicants. Within a few seconds, applications can be reviewed, described to the manager, and screened on the phone. Then, the selected ones can be forwarded by electronic mail or printed out and mailed to the manager. With the old system, the recruiter had to take the order, search through paper files, sometimes find that the file was out with another manager or temporarily misplaced, and eventually, hours later at best, or never at worst, retrieve and ship the file. Now the recruiter can even embed a manager's preferences in the search.

From an operating value standpoint, overtime for administrative support was significantly reduced. The time commitment of hiring managers dropped dramatically. The time needed to fill jobs and the cost per hire also improved. From a public relations point of view, applicants could see that their applications didn't just disappear into a hole. The last person who was the hardest nut to crack became a believer when within a few seconds she was able to retrieve electronically the runner-up for a job filled four months earlier and forward it to the hiring manager for review.

MSKCC was also one of the first companies to put available jobs on a hotline telephone system. After dialing an 800 number, interested persons can use a touch-tone protocol to search job opportunities. This met opposition from those who feared that competitors for the same applicants might somehow subvert the system. That objection was overridden. Once the party has located an interesting position, he or she is instructed to mail in an application or, in special cases, to call a phone number that is supplied. The latest enhancement is a home page wherein an on-line application form can be called up and data entered and transmitted. MSKCC is also putting this capability on other recruitment service company Internet home pages to widen its reach.

MSKCC is one of the most efficient and cost-effective recruiting institutions on the East Coast. Still, it continues to improve and to refine its system. With classified advertising, it puts an identifier on every ad to enable it to do cost/benefit analyses. The data show when is the best time to advertise and when is the worst, such as around a holiday. The system also identifies the yield of low-cost classified ads versus higher-cost display ads.

In our annual research survey of human asset management practices and metrics, we find that, unlike MSKCC's, most recruiting functions have no data on how long it takes to hire, what the cost per hire is, or even the quality of new hires. This is true even where they are using expensive applicant tracking systems. In short, there is a huge gap in management practices between the BHAMs and The Rest.

The Risks and Rewards of Leading

The principal risk of leading is financial. A company can make a large investment that doesn't yield the expected return, thereby crippling it or sometimes driving it into the arms of an acquisitive competitor. Companies who choose to be followers run a safer track but are destined always to be looking at the backside of the leaders. As an earthy Alaskan friend of mine pointed out, "If you are not the lead dog on the team you spend your working life looking up the same arse."

One company shot for the moon by opening up with a high-risk culture. AT&T's Universal Card Services launched its first product in March 1990—the AT&T Universal Card. It was the first card to combine the more traditional credit card services with a long distance calling card.

From the beginning, management openly and strongly encouraged innovation and risk taking. The mandate for everyone is:

❑ *Customer delight.* Don't just satisfy the customers, delight them. Many examples are available, but one makes the point. One associate received a call from a customer who was having car problems and needed help. Why this customer called UCS no one ever asked. On his own, the associate called a member of his family and arranged for a tow truck to pick up the customer.

❑ *Associate delight.* Employees are regarded as crucial to business success. The company's management works to delight the employee "associates" as well. Employees are recognized for exceptional service through the Power of One award created by Fred Winkler, executive vice president for customer service. When the award is due, Fred personally comes into the department with a bull horn to announce it.

❑ *Continuous improvement.* Although the company has done exceptionally well, even winning the Baldrige Award in 1992, it never rests in its search for new and better services. This drive is supported by several internal programs aimed at recognizing improvements. The top of the ladder is the President's Circle. Achievement is based on having demonstrated fulfillment of the company's eight values: customer delight, associate delight, continuous improvement, trust and integrity, a sense of urgency, teamwork, commitment, and mutual respect.

UCS has made risk taking and innovation a cultural mandate. Celebrations are common as associates are recognized for living the cultural norms. Some of the celebration ideas are pretty unusual and might be risky in other companies. Associates might have seen them as silly and a waste of time and money. But management's belief was that if you want something badly enough, you have to take risks to make it happen.

The reward that comes from successful risk taking and innovation is a leading position in your markets. Indicators of market leadership are visible in the form of human, production, and ultimately financial values. Leading in the management of human assets produces higher morale, greater self-confidence and resilience in tough times, more self-direction and problem solving, lower rates of absenteeism and separation, and higher human productivity. Production values enjoyed by the BHAMs are measurable in better-quality products and services, lower unit costs in production, and top-level customer satisfaction. Naturally, these types of values show up on the financial side in increased sales, lower break-even points, larger margins, more retained customers and customer referrals, and market share increases.

Managing the Big Risks

Most firms cannot take on a bet-your-company project. They simply don't have the deep financial pockets that such a risk requires. For them, and they are the vast majority, a different risk strategy is called for. Its name is quantum leap. I referred to it in Chapter 3. Quantum leap is a specific innovation strategy that calls for mentally positioning yourself in the future as the first step.

Having pictured the future to the best of your ability, what do you see as the features of the landscape? What does the marketplace look like? Next, place your company in the picture. Now, what does the company look like in terms of what it must be to succeed? *Be* is the operative term. You have to create a context, not just rearrange some processes. As you mentally look around your future company, what types of words describe it? Look at the structure, systems, and processes, for they are the basis and drivers of employee activity, behavior, and subsequent performance. What are the characteristics of your organizational forms and processes from a human asset management viewpoint? Are they:

flexible	or	fixed
open	or	closed
stimulating	or	deflating
automated	or	manual
participative	or	directed
value-adding	or	transactional
culturally aligned	or	disconnected
uplifting	or	demeaning
customer-focused	or	process-focused

Now, is that the type of organization that you want and that will be effective? If the answers to both questions are yes, then build it now. Don't wait and don't take excuses for answers. Incorporate the naysayers in the process. Lead by example and lend them some of your courage and insights. Remember how the leaders described throughout this book have acted. All of them met resistance. Sometimes they failed, but they never quit.

I am asked continually for the secret of the high-performing companies. It is clearly the personal leadership of one or a few key people who had the vision of the future and wouldn't accept anything less. It took Bob Galvin nearly ten years to change Motorola's culture from paternalistic to participative. Priscilla Smith would not accept the "old Pru" way of doing things. Ed Kleinert had a vision of how automation could improve Memorial Sloan-Kettering's recruitment process. Admiral Hacker at USAA and the top team at AT&T's Universal Cards took the risk of instituting major changes in the way their companies were managed and the new roles that managers and associates would play. In no case did the changes go smoothly. Studies of broad, fundamental change efforts suggest that the road is often extremely long and sure to be filled with many potholes. Only the courageous make it.

Learning Through Risking and Innovating

The key to successful risk taking is quick learning. The smart innovators do their homework. As information and knowledge grow, the risk diminishes. The BHAMs scrutinize the playing field. Customers, competitors, allies and enemies, resource capability and general environmental factors—that is, political, economic, technical, and social dynamics—are studied, learned, and balanced. If appropriate, BHAMs leverage their resources through alliances and partnerships. When it comes to innovating in human asset management, a major consideration is the psyche of the employees who will be affected by the proposed innovation. The same environmental elements apply, but there is a very personal perspective here. Figure 8-1 contains the basic questions to ask yourself when innovating in this area. The rewards of successful innovation are as obvious as its risks. When the innovators win, they win big.

Figure 8-1. Human innovation considerations.

1. Who will be most affected?
2. Where will the effects be found: in job characteristics, pay or benefits, reporting relationships, working relationships, or the physical environment?
3. What might be the perceived personal negatives in the innovation?
4. What are the proposed positives as they affect each person?
5. Why not leave well enough alone? What would be the consequences of not changing?

They spread the field and take a commanding position. This is as it should be. An immutable law of nature is that effort and reward run in parallel. Great, enduring rewards seldom come to those who do not choose to risk and strive.

BHAM Lesson: *Recognize and reward risk taking and you will get innovation.*

A Need for Benchmark Targets

The drive to innovate comes from the desire or need to achieve some type of organizational improvement such as: Increase market share, enter a new market, or reduce operating expense. The objective is often stated either as raising our level of current performance or as achieving or exceeding an external benchmark—usually another company's performance. Normally, the improvement is stated in objective terms. The target serves two purposes. First, it gives direction and a range to the effort, often implying the risk as well. If we are told that the goal is to introduce a new product or service by a certain date, and that if we don't we will lose market share to competitors, the risk is explicit. Second, a performance goal or benchmark target trades on people's natural desire to achieve. Most people want to do well. Many of them want to do better than their competitors. The only ones who eschew competition are those who believe they are going to lose if they play. So, rather than enter the fray, they sit on the sidelines and feign interest in the game. Nevertheless, competition is an inherent human characteristic. It starts with simple survival and can go all the way to full-blown psychotic megalomania. Fortunately, most people are able to keep their competitive instincts within the range of civilized behavior.

Because we all start out wanting to succeed in life we need to know what success looks like. For some it is just a steady job. For others it is a million dollars in the bank. The dreams of success are as many and varied as there are dreamers. Still, all dreamers have a describable goal, a vision. In business we have quantitative goals and objectives. Some are short-term and some are long-range. They are described in terms of cost, time, quantity, quality, or some type of human reaction such as the customer's level of satisfaction with a product or service. In the slower-moving, more stable market-place of the past, innovation was not required if one's goal was simply to survive and reach retirement safely. But in today's market, even survival demands innovation.

One of American companies' major problems is their inability to use quantitative management data effectively. Of course, executives all know how to read their financial statements. But that is the score of *yesterday's* game. They don't do as good a job of developing performance metrics and benchmarks to understand how they are doing *today*, and what data they need *tomorrow*. This is especially true on the human asset side. In general, top management has bought into the legend of the incomprehensibility of human performance measurement. This belief is a self-limiting fabrication of operating managers.

Every function and every process is susceptible to a combination of qualitative and quantitative measures. Internal standards of performance can be set for almost every line and staff task. The problem that people have with measurement is that they focus on what is happening in the process and not on what the desired result should be.

Recently, I was consulting with a company that provides a variety of employee services to large corporations. They offer everything from payroll processing to employee assistance programs. In discussing ways to measure qualitative services such as counseling, they got lost in the process. They wanted to count the number of calls and the average time spent on the phone. That's okay, but those aren't the important issues. What we want to know is what happened as a result of the counseling? In some cases, links can be found to absenteeism, separation rates, cost of treatment, and recidivism levels. External norms can be obtained in some cases. When you measure results, you put the focus on the objective rather than on the process. When introducing an innovation, management must give some type of target that people can see, understand, believe in, and be inspired by. This target must be a value-adding result, not just the completion of the installation of a new process. When the focus is on a benchmark goal that will be measured, everyone's attention is drawn to it. Then, that old axiom comes into play. What gets measured gets done.

The Risk Taker's Checklist

Risk taking must be built into the system. Preaching doesn't do it. If you truly value and desire risk, then make it a part of your culture and design it into your processes. Figure 8-2 is a list of criteria you can use to judge how deeply risk taking and innovation are embedded in your organization.

Summary

If you really want a risk-taking, innovative company, you must embed those characteristics in the culture. You ask for it, you demand it, you use it as your modus operandi in all decision making, you recognize it, you celebrate it.

Building an innovative risk culture means trusting people to try out their ideas without fear of reprisal. Risk taking entails a certain amount of failure. When you fail you must learn from it or be doomed to repeat it. So long as risk and failure drive learning rather than punishment, you have a chance of people taking risks. Recognition does more than anything to stimulate risk-taking behavior. Obviously, successful innovation can be and must be celebrated. But failure should also be presented positively and publicly. There is value in presenting failures to the group. In the course of hearing about a project that failed, someone in the group might have an insight that will turn the failure into a success.

Being a leader is really the only position to play for. The values of being number one or even number two in a market are so much greater than occupying lower rungs on the ladder. In the areas of

Figure 8-2. Risk-taking and innovation checklist.

1. Is innovation explicitly mentioned in the corporate mission statement or other documents dealing with the values of the organization?

2. Does *everyone* have at least one innovation objective in his or her set of performance objectives?

3. Is innovation celebrated openly on every possible occasion?

4. Are attempts at innovation discussed in department meetings?

5. Are failed innovations openly discussed so that others might come up with ideas that will make them work?

6. Are there formal rewards for taking risks and innovating?

7. How many levels of approval are there for new ideas?

8. Are cross-functional teams used to stimulate ideas and share resources?

9. Is there "play money" available to fund innovative ideas in their early stages?

---

human asset management, the leaders enjoy advantages in employee spirit and effort. This leads to faster and cheaper operations that yield higher-quality products and services. Finally, it all hits home with superb financial returns.

The BHAMs are always looking into the future. They have methods for bringing the future to life today. Rather than complain about the barriers to change, they make quantum leaps across the ramparts to "where no one has gone before." Space exploration is risky and rides on innovation, but what a glorious view!

References

1. Edward M. Marshall, *Transforming the Way We Work* (New York: AMACOM, 1995), p. 58.
2. Gifford Pinchot, *Intrapreneuring* (New York: HarperCollins, 1986).

9

Competitive Passion

*How Never Being Satisfied and a
Continuous Improvement Attitude
Keeps the Best Moving Faster
Than the Rest*

Other things being equal, why do the rich continue to get richer? It's because they work at getting richer. So too, the BHAMs work at getting better, faster, so that the gap between them and The Rest continues to widen.

Continuous improvement has become a modern management cliché. It's easy to call for it but not so easy to accomplish. It's natural for all biological organisms from plants to human beings to need periods of rest and recuperation. When I was dabbling in hydroponic farming, I could grow plants all year round in controlled greenhouse conditions. But the perennials needed a rest period. Life is wearing, and growth takes a lot out of the organism. So it is with the corporate body.

Once a group, or even a whole corporation, has achieved a high-level goal, it needs to *take five*. The problem comes when companies try to restart their motors. On the one hand, a success makes everyone feel good and lifts self-confidence. On the other, a counteracting force suggests that they leave well enough alone and rest a while longer.

The secret code for keeping the organization operating at the highest possible level is to build into the system a set of energizing beliefs and disciplines. These describe the nature of the institution that you are attempting to build, sustain, and improve. The key word is *institution*.

An institution is something that endures. It is more than a place that is driving to increase sales. There are many famous institutional companies. These are the ones that have been at the top of their industry for decades. They are the models we always refer to when we want an example of exceptional performance or exceptional citizenship. The institutional approach provides the foundation for long-term, continuous, never-satisfied action.

The antithesis of the institution is a company that simply has a five-year goal to achieve some level of financial growth. Is it a coincidence that the typical tenure of a CEO in the United States is about four to five years? There is nothing wrong with financial growth. But, as we have seen in icons such as Motorola, Hewlett-Packard, General Electric, Procter and Gamble, and, until recently, IBM, they exist for more than financial gain.

PROTECTIVE LIFE

Protective Life Corporation was founded in 1907 to provide financial security through life and health insurance and investment products. Headquartered in Birmingham, Alabama, it has operations throughout the Southeast, parts of the Midwest, and in California. Protective integrates its vision, values, and quality beliefs through five cardinal principles:

1. Focus on the customer.
2. Continuously improve.
3. Equip, empower, and liberate people and trust their capability and willingness to improve quality.
4. Concentrate on the long term, the whole process, and the team.
5. Use statistical analysis to understand and continuously improve the process.

The notion of continuous improvement is operationalized through operating policies and systems and the company's treatment of people. Systems and culture drive the required human behavior that results in the performance desired. Protective starts the process at the point of hire. It puts a great deal of effort into recruitment and selection. Its belief is that picking the right person in the beginning not only stimulates top-quality performance, it also creates high morale and cuts down on turnover.

Protective's beliefs are played out by staffing practices that revolve around finding a "best fit" for each position. Specifically, this means looking inside first because there the person already fits and has a personal commitment to the company. Second, it means hiring quality rather than quantity. Third, it calls for testing applicants for desired skills rather than relying only on interviews and résumés. Fourth, it involves creating profiles of the kind of personality and characteristics that have proven to be requisite for the job. Next, it means communicating extensively and effectively, and, finally, using the PIT Crew.

Protective's policy has always been to hire from within whenever possible. Counting all vacant positions, about one-third are filled from within, and if entry-level jobs are subtracted, that figure more than doubles. The usual hiring tactics, such as job posting, are applied. Beyond that, Protective has a program that encourages people to move horizontally as well as vertically. This provides many people with a broad array of skills and experience. Because of this practice most professional and managerial positions can be filled from within the current employee population. The majority of outside hiring is done at the lower levels or when specialized, technical skills are required.

More than a dozen years ago the claims department decided that to cut expenses it would hire the lowest-cost claims examiners it could find. This flew in the face of Protective's beliefs. It was penny-wise and pound-foolish. It ignored the value-adding side in favor of an expense-reduction-only approach. After reviewing the work, management decided that claims should hire half as many claims adjusters, but bring in only the best available, and use lower-paid administrative personnel to handle the routine paperwork. Although there was some concern about this approach, the strategy was followed. Subsequent monitoring showed that this method produced better customer service, lowered turnover, and reduced training costs.

Protective puts a great deal of effort into ensuring employee fit.

This is common among the best performing companies. Multiple interviews are more the rule here than the exception. In this case, the hiring process is divided into three phases. After the initial screening of applicants to produce candidates, basic skills tests are administered. These relate to the skill requirements of the open position. The tests can include reading comprehension, math, and perceptual or analytical abilities. In addition, all applicants are asked to write on the backs of their tests why they want to work at Protective. This provides a sample of the person's communication skills.

The second phase depends on the position in question. It might involve role-playing of a situation that the candidate would typically be confronted with on the job. Here the person's thought processes and behavior under stress can be seen.

In the third phase, candidates are tested for cultural fit. Personality tests are given for managerial positions. An outside firm evaluates the results. In the case of a senior management position, the candidate will spend half a day with Protective's industrial psychologist.

In all, the psychological profile fit consists of a structured interview, a biographical profile, and appropriate testing of mental and personality traits. This three-phase method gives the company information on skill sets, analytic and problem-solving capability, and personality traits.

Collaboration comes into play in the communications strategy. Each week Bill Hammer, vice president of human resources, meets with those reporting to him to review staffing for the past week and to look ahead. They periodically monitor staffing trends over the past five years. Each quarter the staff reviews whichever business unit hired the most people during that period. It gathers data on the number of new hires and the reasons for their being hired. Then, meetings are held with senior management to discuss staffing objectives. Information from many of these processes is communicated to all employees directly and through their involvement in the PIT Crew.

The PIT Crew is composed of volunteer employees who have had at least three years' experience at Protective. Team membership is for one year. The Crew uses formal feedback devices such as employee surveys, interviews, and financial data, as well as informal employee comments. They meet quarterly to develop action teams as needed. The principal responsibility of the PIT Crew is to develop information on specific programs and issues from the employees and feed it back into the system. This mechanism ensures that top management always hears the voice of the people.

The strong emphasis on effective staffing has produced a number of qualitative and quantitative values for the company. Protective Life's financial performance compares very favorably with the average for the financial services industry. Hiring time and turnover rates are as much as two-thirds lower than industry norms. When the volume of new hires rose dramatically in the early 1990s, the efficiencies that had been introduced into the process allowed the company to handle this load with no increase in the hiring staff. One of the most telling observations came from CEO Drayton Nabers, when commenting on the use of hard data to manage the hiring function: "This is a fine example of the kind of objective and quantitative information that we can have in a part of the company which many think involves only qualitative and soft factors."

Disconnects

Edward M. Marshall suggests that managing a transition process is like managing a marriage.[1] It is a permanent assumption and it takes a lot of work. The same principle applies to continuous improvement. Underlying the employee-company relationship is a type of integrity that is built on the expressed values of the company. To make continuous improvement a way of life, it first has to exist as a value that pervades all aspects of the corporate body. Improvement activities must then follow those values. This is operationalized along four interfaces: leadership, business and customers, work force relationships, and organizational systems.

The disconnect occurs when there is a noticeable gap between what top management says it wants, or is committed to, and what actually happens. A typical example occurs when an executive charges his employees with a new vision or a new activity, vows to be involved and to support the drive, then quickly disappears from the arena. When confronted, such executives claim that they are too busy to attend to everything. The employees know better. Figure 9-1 shows the interfaces and the actions required at each.

Disconnects create myriad elemental problems that are very difficult to overcome. When executives lose contact with their peo-

Figure 9-1. Managing the interfaces.

Interface	Requirements
Leadership	Keep your word. Commit yourself and your company to success. Lead by example. Be open to changing your own behavior.
Business and Customer	Make integrity the cornerstone of customer relations. Build an institution that makes everyone proud. Keep the customer uppermost in your mind. Give full value at all times. Go beyond customer requirements.
Work Force Relationships	Support skill development. Require continuous personal growth. Encourage risking and learning. Make innovation the purpose of work. Forgive failure. Recognize and celebrate successes.
Organization Processes and Systems	Simplify processes. Design humanistic systems. Build a communications network and use it. Craft a continuous improvement culture.

ple and with the improvement process, they have breached integrity and are no longer leaders. Forgetting or losing interest in customer needs results in customers firing the company. This not only affects sales in the short term, it also requires expensive concessions to win back the customer. If this goes on long enough, it damages the firm's reputation, and loss of reputation is the greatest loss of all.

One way the company can show interest in both its customers and employees is by providing training and opportunities for growth. This includes career discussions that confirm that the company has not forgotten its people. Failure to maintain this connection leads to apathy, eventually anger, and in some cases voluntary separation. Throughout the process of disconnection, the employee's output slows down, errors tend to rise, and customers don't receive the level of service they previously enjoyed.

Finally, since processes and systems dictate behavior, it is important to view the workplace from the employees' standpoint. Does the organization help or hinder human effort? Are the systems controlling or supportive? Are communication channels both open and their use encouraged? Is the performance management system punitive or constructive? Has management given people the tools they need to do their jobs?

BE PREPARED

The Boy Scouts of America was founded in 1910 and currently has more than 4 million members. The National Council employs 1,200 people at its headquarters in Irving, Texas, and eight other locations around the country. The staff practices the famous Boy Scouts's motto, "Be Prepared," in its own work.

Because BSA is a nonprofit organization, it has to be particularly careful how it spends its money. The staff is constantly on the lookout for ways to improve its operations. In the early 1990s, it instituted changes in the health plan regarding the purchase of prescription drugs by employees. Traditionally, the BSA paid retail prices for the medications. But as prices continued to rise, it looked for ways to control the expense. The organization held negotiations with eight pharmaceutical vendors and decided to go with a mail order plan for long-term maintenance drugs. The vendor agreed to meet performance targets for generic fill rates and costs. The first year the vendor missed the target and paid a penalty fee of $25,000 to the Boy Scouts. The next year the vendor improved but still had to pay. Overall, the program saved the BSA and its employees and retirees $270,000 annually.

In its pursuit of continuous improvement, the BSA automated many procedures. As a result, it was able to conduct more accurate analyses of various programs. In the case of health insurance services, it detected a discrepancy of a half million dollars in the year-end financial accounting received from one of the carriers. The error was presented to the carrier, which at first did not agree. However, further investigation and review proved the mistake and a check for $500,000 was given to the Scouts. By constantly looking for ways to improve employee services and still cut costs, the BSA has proved itself perennially to be a well-managed operation.

First Tennessee

First Tennessee Bank is a holding company headquartered in Memphis, Tennessee. The company, through its various local banking systems, operates in twenty-five states. In the face of the trend toward creation of megabank corporations, First Tennessee has to be extraordinarily efficient to compete with the larger-scale operations of the giants.

With service as the principal competitive advantage in banking, FTB relies on a full-staffing philosophy. For Pat Brown in the bank's human resources function, this means that when a job becomes vacant in a branch bank, she wants it filled immediately with a qualified person. The standard for filling teller-level positions in banks in the Midwest has averaged twenty-four days over the past five years.

At FTB, they aim to beat that number by a wide margin. One method they have used to attack the problem is to establish their own talent pool. They encourage job applicants to take part-time jobs or to join the bank's temporary pool when full-time positions are not available. This gives the bank a list of prequalified people who are ready and able to go to work overnight. Some of them already have experience with the bank's systems and just have to switch from part-time to full-time status. In turn, they are replaced by someone from the pool. With these types of jobs, 93 percent are filled through this pool service.

The pool is part of FTB's Rapid Applicant Processing system. RAP is more than a slick acronym for a fast processing function. It is an integration of applicant flow management, recruitment management, work force planning, quality improvement, and the internal temporary placement service. Such an integrated, holistic approach is rare. Features include a tightly scheduled applicant processing procedure lasting no more than two to three hours. Within this time, a lot happens:

- ❑ Applicants complete the job application.
- ❑ Applicants take a validated skills test.
- ❑ HR reviews the application and test results.
- ❑ The hiring manager interviews the top candidates.

❑ A drug test and reference check are conducted on the selected candidate(s).

The testing program has increased employee quality by 20 percent. Validated tests have been developed for all nonexempt candidates. The testing program is kept up to date through ongoing correlations of test scores and on-the-job performance evaluations. The tests screen for ability to learn, work orientation, dependability, self-esteem, interpersonal skills, customer service aptitudes, and sales ability.

To continue to improve its service, First Tennessee introduced a job hotline and posted job openings both internally and with 100 selected external organizations. Through this publicity, the bank has become recognized as a highly effective recruiting machine. As a result, other companies came to the bank and asked it to help them fill their temporary positions. In final tally, First Tennessee's devotion to continually improving its recruitment function has shortened the time it takes to fill jobs by 35 percent, cut the cost of hiring by more than 60 percent of the industry standard, and increased the quality of the people hired.

Paranoia or Common Sense?

There is more than one way to look at the phenomenon of never being satisfied. A cynic might say it is a symptom of corporate paranoia. Maybe it is. But if so, it is a useful mental aberration. Looking over your shoulder at who might be approaching or attacking your market is one way of not being startled. It keeps you safe from sudden surprise attacks. When you maintain a good scanning system, you usually see farther into the future than others do. This helps to distance your company from the competition.

Looking back to see if someone is gaining on you can be confounded by the historic fact that in most cases the quantum leaps made within an industry or a market segment have come from outsiders. The insiders who were leading the pack were usually somewhere between complacent and arrogant. This, of course, is when they were most vulnerable to attack from an unseen quarter.

Consider a few of the major product and service breakthroughs of the past thirty years. Where did personal computers come from? Not from IBM, which had 60 percent of the computing market in the 1970s. Two kids named Steve cooked up a new version of the idea that earlier entrepreneurs had introduced but never successfully commercialized. Apple Computer was already a billion-dollar business before IBM was able to answer the challenge to its minicomputer business.

Who thought up an overnight package delivery service? It wasn't anyone inside the postal service, freight, or transportation industries. A guy named Smith, Fred to be exact, founded Federal Express. The efficient mini-steel mill didn't come from U.S. Steel or Bethlehem Steel. Portable cellular telephones were not popularized by any of the telephone companies. Bioengineering didn't come from one of the old-line pharmaceutical companies.

Take a look over your shoulder. Is there anyone out there with a crazy idea that could upset your wagon? If there is, this person is probably not currently a major player in your industry.

Sources for Improvement Ideas

Most of the best ideas I get don't come from focusing on human asset management. They come from outside the box sources. Reading in information technology or finance helps because I believe that technology, finance, and people can and must work together more effectively. I pick up insights from reading history, true adventures, economics, and physics. I've gained new perspectives that apply to managing the human side of organizations from reading Eastern philosophy. The key is to reserve judgment, let the underlying themes sink in, and try to find a kernel of relevant truth that applies across disciplines. Even essentially negative views such as those found in *The Art of War* or *The Secrets of Attila the Hun* offer different perspectives that can be turned into positive applications. We can't make discoveries by looking at the old ways. Looking outside our field drives us down new paths to better ways of managing our human assets. It leads us to new solutions for stimulating human productivity and improving employee morale or loyalty.

Lessons From Cultural Anthropology

An example of how to gain knowledge in one area that can be used in another would be reading about cultural differences across nations. Fons Trompenaars described differences in culture types by contrasting ways of relating to people and classifying them into five comparative sets.[2] Figure 9-2 displays the differences.

How does this knowledge apply to learning for continuous improvement? It would be a mistake to focus it exclusively on the subject of diversity management. In my not very humble opinion, the principles of diversity management are a combination of the Golden Rule and common sense. If you have a group of people that comes from a distinctive ethnic or cultural background, it is ridiculous to ignore the fact that these people will see the world from their own perspective. While they may share some views, they also have others that are unique to their particular culture.

Figure 9-2. Contrasting cultural views on five dimensions of human relationship.

Universalism: What is good and right can be defined and is always applicable.

Particularism: Friendship is a special obligation and may take precedence over an abstract societal code of conduct.

Individualism: It is most important to be what and who I am.

Collectivism: It is more important to consider the group first.

Neutrality: Relationships are detached and instrumental, aimed at achieving objectives.

Emotionalism: Business is a human affair in which emotional displays are natural.

Specificity: The relationship is defined by the issue and should stay focused on that.

Diffuseness: The personal relationship itself is the basis on which the business is built.

Achievement: Judgments of worth are based on recent accomplishments and on one's record.

Ascription: Status is based on birth, kinship, gender, age, and connections.

Source: Adapted from Fons Trompenaars, *Riding the Waves of Culture* (London: Irwin, 1993), p. 10.

Because all of us naturally look at the world through our own little windows, we tend to narrow our field of vision. This means that we see only in a limited way. Studying other cultures and listening to people of different cultural backgrounds brings these differences to the surface and makes us think about ways of relating to them.

The prime question is: How does one reconcile cultural diversity with competitive passion? Are we into the nature-nurture argument at a more complex level? Are some cultures not naturally competitive, or are they just victims of centuries of domination that have robbed them seemingly of a motivation to be the best? I'm not qualified to argue either side of that issue. Yet, from an organizational management, continuous improvement perspective, we must consider the effect of culture on competitiveness. In short, it seems that any group, company, or nation that does not choose to compete, study, and constantly improve dooms itself to a very poor existence.

As one example, let me cite New Zealand. I have made a number of trips to New Zealand over the past decade. In the 1980s, I perceived the country to be populated by wishful thinkers. They seemed to me to want to ignore the rest of the world, and especially some of the less attractive aspects of the Northern Hemisphere. It looked to me as if they yearned to live in a pre–World War II world. As a result, their political and economic policies were rather introspective. This caused a long-term recession that lasted well into the 1990s. During a visit in mid-1996, I noticed an entirely different attitude. The government had taken some necessary but not very palatable steps to reform their economy. Businesspeople accepted that they had to compete or drop back into a Third World economy. To their credit, they turned the country around. The attitudes I encountered were entirely different, much more positive, and even contentious, to the degree that those nice people can be contentious.

My principal conclusion from this and other experiences outside of the United States causes me to believe that personal pride and competition are natural human traits. So the good news is that if approached properly, managers can expect people to continually improve their performance. The other conclusion is that we have to take everyone as they are and look for the most effective way to unleash the competitive passion, whether it be with our own people or with foreign nationals. The study of cultural anthropology is an example of how data from a seemingly unconnected discipline can be applied to managing business enterprises and helping them improve. It shouldn't be surprising because managing human assets is all about understanding how people react to their environment.

First, an appreciation of cultural factors might help us to manage our own diverse work forces more effectively. Second, it will help us to understand how to do business with people from other cultures. With the global marketplace, improvement ideas can be found anywhere. To be so different as to be distinct, a person doesn't have to have another skin color, an unusual religious belief, or live thousands of miles away. In a country as large as the United States, there are obvious regional differences. Texans certainly look at life differently from the way Bostonians do. People from Georgia to Virginia march to a different drummer than the one followed by people from New Jersey, although southern Jersey is only a couple of hundred miles from northern Virginia. The biggest gap is probably between Midwesterners in the Plains states and Californians. Our many subcultures offer something of value in decision making.

Of course, culture variation plays an even larger role when we cross oceans. I'm made aware of these differences whenever I train, or attempt to train, people in other countries in methods of quantitative evaluation. It isn't that they can't do the statistics involved. It's that they have a way of looking at human performance and recognition that is more subjective than the one I'm describing. Family-based societies such as the Malaysian are driven by different motivations than those most common to individualistic Americans. The question for them is not *how* to measure something but rather *why* it is necessary to use such measures or *what* is to be done if performance does not meet the standard. From that I've learned how to present objective analysis in a personal manner. I've also come to understand how to do business with them. I realize that we have to establish a personal relationship first. I have to spend time with them and try to meet their families.

In other family-based countries such as Mexico, I've learned that I might be invited to someone's home for a drink or dinner.

But I'm not a full and true compadre until I'm invited into the kitchen to sit around the table. I've also learned that if I encourage people to talk while I listen appreciatively, we get along better than if I start pitching my ideas and agenda immediately. The destination of best human asset management can be reached by many paths.

FROM BEGINNING TO END

Lutheran General Hospital was founded in 1959, and is located in Park Ridge, Illinois, a suburb of Chicago. It employs 4,000 people and is part of the Lutheran General Health System, which includes hospitals, addiction treatment centers, and retirement and assisted-living centers. Lutheran Hospital, recently merged into Gundersen Lutheran in LaCrosse, Wisconsin, now is part of a large, complex, medical service company. It manages five hospitals, thirty clinics, group homes, vision and sports medicine centers, and employs 6,200 people. The two organizations share a name but are different corporate entities. Together, they show how best practices can function in comparable facilities, providing similar services, located in different communities.

Hospital management is known for its attention to detail. Planning and monitoring are a continuous partnering operation among finance, human resources, and line management. These functions analyze vacancy rates, absenteeism, turnover and compensation trends, exit interview data, and employee comments. This constant analysis and evaluation attempts to keep the hospital ahead of problems, and helps it manage operating costs. In Park Ridge, the Lutheran General Hospital system runs on five core values: respect, service, stewardship, creativity, and collaboration. Senior Vice President John Eiden believes that the hospital's success is driven by a combination of the five values and employee involvement.

For many years, Lutheran General's staff has devoted itself to continually improving the entire range of human asset management. Years ago, they started by flowcharting every activity in the human resource function. The first objective was to separate value-adding activities from those that were simply a cost of doing business. As one example, typical of many organizations, they discovered that twelve monthly reports, carrying duplicate data, were circulating in the company. To cap the inefficiency, the terms in one report were defined differently from the same terms in another report. It was a modern Tower of Babel. By partnering with the line managers, they were able to reduce this mass of literature to eight reports—all driven by terms that were commonly defined and agreed to. This one action eliminated the need for and the cost of three-quarters of the work of one position. This is a classic example of continuous improvement. It is not always a bold stroke that wipes out whole functions. But it is always a value-adding result.

Recruiting is an important issue at Lutheran General, as it was in several other cases. The BHAMs understand how critical the hiring process is to all future activities and results. Time spent in selecting the right person for the job pays off a hundredfold in fewer employee problems, lower turnover, higher productivity, and better customer service. At the time of application, Lutheran General's candidates are evaluated on the basis of a behaviorally anchored selection system. The screening interview questions pull out the candidates' values, technical skills, and experience levels. These data are then entered into a database and correlated with a matrix to determine best fit. Gains have been documented in improved applicant-to-hire ratios, increased productivity, reduced absenteeism and turnover, and increased patient satisfaction.

Compensation is another area that closely involves both line and staff management. At budgeting time, Lutheran General does not play budget Ping-Pong. This is the game of sending in a fat budget, getting back management's required cuts, sending in the next version, getting that back with more cuts, and so on until, through sheer exhaustion, everyone agrees to live with a budget that no one likes. At Lutheran, the human resources staff provides line with the staffing and compensation data needed to develop workable budgets. Budget requests can then be based on solid data rather than wishes or guesses. The end result is a much less time-consuming process, and one that yields figures to which all can be committed. This is only possible because the staff monitors staffing and compensation costs continuously. They know what it costs to hire someone and to provide total pay and benefits for a given class of positions.

Employee turnover can be a huge hidden cost. On average, the voluntary separation of a nonexempt employee costs a company at least six months' salary. Highly skilled professional and managerial positions can easily cost in excess of two years in pay if there are relocations and long learning curves involved. Most hospitals are particularly susceptible to turnover because skilled medical personnel are often in short supply. During the 1980s, Lutheran Hospital in LaCrosse had lived with an 18 percent turnover rate in special skill jobs such as physical and occupational therapy, pharmaceuticals, and nursing. Management decided to attack the retention problem on several fronts simultaneously. To start with, it reviewed its compensation and benefits package to make sure it was competitive. Then, it launched programs in educational reimbursement, flextime options, positive discipline, leadership development, and peer performance review.

As is the case in most BHAM companies, Lutheran LaCrosse formed an employee committee to evaluate the way programs are designed and implemented. This advisory committee is a cross-functional team that meets quarterly. It has representatives from all departments, and members can serve for one or two years. The committee surveys employees for feedback on policies and programs, and makes recommendations to management. This doesn't result in a blank check. In several cases, the employees asked for benefits or programs that subsequent investigation showed did not make economic sense. In others, the services were already available in one form or another, but employees were unaware of them.

In 1990, the hospital launched its Leadership Development Program. This was led by Vice President Bill Schrum, and focused on the 150-person management group. It began with a pilot program and follow-on review by a management committee. After running for three years, it was expanded to include supervisors and other professional-level employees. In 1994, an external consultant was hired to conduct an in-depth evaluation of the program. As a result, the program is continually improved on the basis of hard and soft data.

Underlying the whole effort is a desire to build career plans for management personnel. An assessment and peer review process provides input that people can use to acquire or improve their skills. Short- and long-term goals are set. Finally, ten measures of leadership were identified by Lutheran's supervisory and management staff. Then, a set of performance standards and measures was developed. This system continued to be improved and worked into daily operations. Using work teams formed around the system of standards, measures, and peer reviews, the hospital got its major problems addressed, and its people built skills. By the mid 1990s, Lutheran's turnover rate had dropped by 50 percent.

The lesson in this case of parallel organizations is that whether you're operating in a major metropolitan area like Park Ridge or a smaller municipality in a more rural environment like LaCrosse, the basic principles of effective management are the same.

Keeping a Jump Ahead

Another tactic that is used to keep a step ahead of the competition is to be constantly looking for new customer opportunities. This is more than just expanding an existing customer base by selling more of the same product. It requires looking for the needs of a customer that does not presently exist. Nicholas Imparato and Oren Harai[3]: talk about it as "looking a customer ahead." It makes sense. While we don't want to ignore our current customers, growth demands that we look into the distance, over the horizon, to what might be. The way this plays on the management front is to shift attention from cost cutting and process improvement to revenue generation through innovation. Cutting the expense line is good, but it will not grow the company. Many companies have reached the point of diminishing returns from staff reductions. This takes care of the cost side. But now they need to move across the ledger to the revenue column. To look ahead, organizations should employ a three-step strategy:

1. *Vision.* Start by reexamining the corporate and the staff visions. We recommend that the vision be reviewed annually as the starting point for new growth.

2. *Opportunity search.* The next step is to research the market for new opportunities, for needs customers themselves don't even realize they have. How many people thought they had to have a hand-held calculator in the 1960s or a personal computer in the 1970s? Was anyone crying for overnight package delivery or portable telephones? Cutting the expense side didn't create any of these products. At best, cost cutting and process improvement buy time and might save capital that can be put into market research and product development.

3. *Commitment.* Given an insight into what a new offering might bring, everything should be thrown into getting to market first. This isn't done with some complex planning program that takes weeks or months to design. Instead, each function has a natural responsibility and accountability. Line managers should look ahead to their staffing requirements and get them into the recruiters' hands ASAP. Recruiters should focus on time and quality as their hiring imperatives. Compensation should put together incentive plans to stimulate responsiveness throughout the organization. Training needs to get critical skills honed pronto. Information services prepares reporting and analysis programs to monitor progress. Accounting sets up a budget system. Purchasing procures the needed materials in time for each phase of development. In short, a concerted team effort must be organized and coordinated quickly to reduce any slippage in the organizational machinery.

The value of being first to market cannot be overstated. The penalty for being late to the market will be paid in diminished returns for the life of the product. Beating the competition to market often requires new structures and processes. It calls for the leveraging capability of electronic technology. It might even mean introducing speed into a deliberate culture.

When your company adopts the looking-ahead approach, it positions itself to define the market on its own terms. This is what I referred to earlier as future architecturing. It means you set customer expectations in a way that can only be well served by yourself. You establish your product or service as the model that others are forced to copy. But while others are busy copying version one, your company is working on version two. You may not lock up the market, but at least you're the first one to get your hands on the keys.

> **BHAM Lesson:** *The only position to occupy is first; if we don't do it, someone else will.*

Competitive Passion

Developing a never satisfied or continuous improvement list is easy. There are two key standards of performance—your company and your competition. There are two time frames—present and future. The basic questions are:

1. *What is our performance?* Consider each key function: production, sales, customer service, information technology, research and development, finance and accounting, human resources, and so on. The performance can be described in the three central objectives of a business unit, whether it be line or staff: productivity, quality, and service. Improvements in the central three are measurable by a combination of cost, time, volume, errors, and human reactions. This was described in Chapter 2 and outlined in Figure 2-2. Use the value cell matrix as a template to put over every job and unit. Select the performance levels that, if met or exceeded, would lead to competitive advantage for your company. Monitor those indices at least quarterly. If you have chosen wisely, you will have an effective set of current performance measures.

2. *How do we compare?* Obtain data on your competitors or on functions like yours in other companies not in your industry. If you want to be the best, and who wouldn't, you should be benchmarking the world-class standards. Just be sure that the data you are gathering or reviewing are valid. They must be supported by an objective base and a standard methodology.

3. *How well are we prepared for the future?* It is fine to be performing well now, but what about tomorrow? Design some leading indicators that tell you if you are ready for whatever might be coming. Indices here would come principally from the world of intellectual capital. These include human, process, information, innovation, and organizational capabilities. You might monitor competency, commitment, retention, leadership, and succession tables for the human side. In process, you ought to be looking into technological issues that will give you an edge in productivity, quality, or service delivery. Information has to do with your ability to acquire, develop, and, most important, utilize data effectively. Innovation is obviously your ability to deliver leading-edge products and services as shown by sales of new products. Finally, organizational adaptability and flexibility is a function of your systems and policies.

Knowing where you are now, how you compare with the best in class, and how well you are positioned for whatever the future will bring should be enough to keep you from ever being content or arrogant. Don't forget, when someone blocks new ideas with the "How do you argue with success?" argument, remind him of all the great companies that have failed. Every year there are winners and losers. You have no guarantee that next year you will be a winner unless you are willing to do what others are doing and do it better.

Summary

Looking ahead for what's necessary to do to lead in the future is a hallmark of the BHAMs. Never being satisfied avoids the complacency of success. So many executives who drive their companies to a dominant market position become arrogant. Their favorite audience response is, "How can you argue with success?" The answer is, "It's easy. That was yesterday and we are only going to get paid for what we do tomorrow." In 1995, gross sales of fifty-seven of the Forbes 500 declined from the previous year. Ninety-four saw their profits fall. And eighty-one watched their assets shrink.

Continuous improvement is driven by the institutional value of never being satisfied. It's part of the culture of the BHAMs. Nothing is sacred in these firms. Everyone knows that they can and should be reviewing all processes all the time. This constant pressure to improve yields a continuous stream of small and sometimes large reductions in expense or increases in productivity, quality, or service.

Disconnections can stop improvement programs before they get out of the blocks. Worse than that, they can virtually destroy a company. Disconnection is caused by the actions of the leadership. The top executives have to live the improvement imperative. Their behavior must model never being satisfied. They recognize, celebrate, and reward improvements, then say, "What are we going to do to top that?" Disconnects occur when the CEO or the top management team loses contact with the customers or the employees. If they disconnect from the employees, their integrity is damaged; they lose their loyalty and sabotage their motivation to innovate or produce. When they disconnect from the market and their customers, they lose their shirt. Disconnections are not inevitable at all. But they are so important that the top team must constantly monitor its own behavior—because the employees certainly are.

Although some might say that never being satisfied is a form of corporate paranoia, I would point out that those who become complacent quickly lose their place in line. The marketplace is not disposed to protect anyone. It accepts whoever performs best. In many cases, major breakthroughs have come from someone outside the market. Perhaps it takes an outsider to see the possibilities. Or the outsider may be frustrated by an unmet need. No matter what the reason, the wise executive splits the corporate intelligence unit into both monitoring the current market and simultaneously looking outside the market for crazy ideas that are just starting to attract attention.

Ideas for improvement often come from outside the box in which we find ourselves. By exposing our group to material from other disciplines and cultures we improve the odds of coming up with new ideas. Everyone has a potential for some amount of creativity. That potential can be released through exposure to new ideas. Meeting different kinds of people, reading, listening to speakers, or using other forms of contact with nonmanagement material can be eye-opening. Insights can be obtained from the physical sciences, philosophy, biographies, or other nonfiction from cultures or countries outside our own. We all need fresh infusions now and then. Getting outside our comfort zone often generates new ideas.

Finally, look a customer ahead if you want to jump ahead. You don't want to ignore your current customers and you don't want to stop your drive to wring greater efficiency out of your existing processes and systems. But if you want to lead the market, you have to look ahead. Three steps will do it: Review your vision annually to stay ahead of the market; constantly search for wild new ideas that can dazzle the market; commit everyone in a concerted effort to get to market first. There is no substitute for leading the market. When you are the leader, you can configure the market to suit your strengths. This helps you to continually widen the gap.

References

1. Edward M. Marshall, *Transforming the Way We Work* (New York: AMACOM, 1995), pp. 165–167.
2. Fons Trompenaars, *Riding the Waves of Culture* (London: Irwin, 1993), p. 10.
3. Nicholas Imparato and Oren Harari, *Jumping the Curve* (San Francisco: Jossey-Bass, 1994).

10

Best Practices Around the World

How the Eight Best Practice Factors Operate Across Borders and Cultures

Once someone discovers a management practice that is effective in one location, the obvious question is: Will it be effective in other regions, countries, and cultures? We have seen such systems as quality circles work very well in Japan but not as well without modification in the United States. The work cells found in Swedish factories didn't go over very well in American manufacturing plants either. On the other hand, the impersonal Yankee reengineering approach doesn't work well in Asian and Hispanic companies, which operate according to a different interpersonal ethic. In Chapter 9 we looked briefly at the differences between such cultural values as individualism versus collectivism and achievement versus ascription. It is clear that the one-size management tool does not fit all organizations. Therefore, is it reasonable to expect BHAM principles to work around the world or not? The answer, as you will see in the following cases, is yes, with cultural adaptations.

Our Research Base

The Saratoga Institute's research covers nearly twenty countries. We asked the managing directors in several of the countries in our

Saratoga Global Network to look into the application of BHAM principles in these countries. After conducting their studies, they came up with the following conclusion:

BHAM principles apply in every country studied with the following qualification. Factor by factor, there are many examples of their applicability and efficacy. However, local customs, regulations, economic and social conditions, and business cultural traditions mold the factors in unique ways.

As you will see, when foreigners deal with the eight BHAM factors, they activate them in ways that fit their culture. As the saying goes, "business is business," but it doesn't dress the same in every country. Many local managers have found that they could import foreign operating systems, but if they wanted to be extraordinarily successful, they had to modify the tool to meet local needs and expectations. The latest example of this phenomenon is China. Although the leaders of the People's Republic are desperate for investment capital to create jobs, Chinese managers have found that Western methods can't be absorbed as readily as its capital. Even overseas Chinese, when seconded to the mainland, do not always know the most effective way to supervise their cousins. Briefly, we found these variations:

❑ *Values.* Human and financial values are appreciated in all cultures. However, in some, the economic situation is such that financial survival is paramount. Where that is not the case, human value is expressed in national terms that often differ across borders.

❑ *Commitment.* Enterprises that build for the long term are more successful in every situation. This is particularly true in highly volatile countries like Venezuela, Brazil, and, lately, Mexico. In extreme circumstances, when others are falling right and left, the enterprise builders tend to fare better because they have stronger foundations of loyalty and creativity. An apparent exception would be a trading center like Hong Kong, where entrepreneurs are buying and selling businesses and property, often with great success. However, these people are traders, not managers.

The only enterprise they want to build is their personal net worth. Their objectives are short-term. It does them no good to grow organizations for the future because they won't be there.

❑ *Culture.* This is the most idiosyncratic of the factors. The volatile and engaging Brazilians are certainly different from the reserved Swiss and English. The Malaysians are much more devoted to family and personal factors than are American individualists. Nevertheless, in all cases we found that the BHAM companies actively managed their culture and linked it with their operating and administrative systems. This is particularly evident in the collective cultures in which personal relationships mean so much. In these, systems and rewards are very purposely designed to support and strengthen relationships and mutual respect. This value means that when times are tough everyone who feels valued will endure great hardships as part of the collective.

❑ *Partnering.* Here we find the most basic diversity. Partnering fits better in collective cultures except where there is a strong hierarchical system. Places like Mexico and Germany, where there is traditionally strong respect for authority, find partnering somewhat unusual. They are used to having someone give direction. On the other hand, younger generations are less apt to be as obedient as their parents were. This is especially true in Japan, where the miracle of Japan's success was wrung from the devotion of workers to the national cause. Japanese companies are now trying to find a new emblem around which to rally the more individualistic new generation. We expect that partnering will become more common in formerly collective cultures in the near future.

❑ *Collaboration.* This is a mirror image of partnering, only more so. Where partnering is more common, collaboration is very prominent. Where partnering is a new idea, collaboration hardly exists. In effect, collaboration is a microcosmic example of partnering. It is carried along by the power of the partnering ethic.

❑ *Innovation and risk.* Some cultures are very risk-averse overall, yet that doesn't mean they sit on their hands. In Asia, businesspeople usually have their bases well covered when they launch a new venture. They are less likely to take a flyer than are some others, like the Australian or American entrepreneurs of the 1980s.

Many of those high-leverage players from Donald Trump to Kerry Packer blazed like rockets before fizzling out. In cultures in which there is great respect for tradition, authority, and the feelings of others, we find less innovation. Still, there was a significant level of innovation and risk apparent in all organizations studied. The differential across borders is only one of degree.

❑ *Competitive passion.* In today's market, no matter where you site your business, if you become content, satisfied, or complacent, you don't maintain market share for long. When someone says to you, "Why should I change? How can you argue with success?" you know you are looking at a person who is about to be overtaken by his competitors. With the world now one big marketplace, everyone in it is vying for everyone else's customers and jobs. All organizations, including governmental offices, are struggling down the road of continuous improvement. The BHAMs are most notable for their constant striving to better themselves.

Industrial Applications

This chapter provides case studies of six organizations, representing several private and public entities.

Country	Organization	Industrial Classification
Australia	Queensland Treasury	State government
Canada	Canadian Imperial Bank of Commerce	Finance
Mexico	Cigatam	Consumer products
New Zealand	Griffins Foods	Consumer products
United Kingdom	British Airways	Transportation
Venezuela	Pequiven	Petrochemicals

BRITISH AIRWAYS
LONDON, ENGLAND

Transformation

In the early to mid-1980s, British Airways was in a highly distressed position. It was losing approximately £200 per minute, and for the year 1981–82 declared an overall deficit of £544 million. This included special provisions to pay for an extensive *survival plan* that required staff cuts of around 20,000, suspension of unprofitable routes, and the disposal of BA's surplus assets. The project of reestablishing the company was launched in 1983 under the direction of Colin Marshall with the goal of repositioning the carrier as the "World's Favourite Airline."

Four years later, in 1987, British Airways was privatized and a merger with British Caledonian announced. This carried with it a number of cultural as well as business implications. Over the past decade a wide range of initiatives has assisted in positioning British Airways as a world-class multinational business. Many of these have been people initiatives. Training has been one area that has been highly influential in changing staff behavior, improving customer service, raising organizational competence, and generally reinforcing the best practice characteristics of BHAM companies within BA.

Training's Role in the Transformation

Early on, Marshall recognized that people, not aircraft, were the differentiating feature of an airline. To help rescue the company, he instilled a sense of partnering between management and employees. Passenger service, on-time arrival, and patient handling of unforeseeable problems, he thought, could renew the airline. Marshall decreed and funded a development system for all employees, and over the past twelve years core training and development programs have been designed for all 50,000 BA employees around the world. They have been aimed at establishing and strengthening the behaviors required by a leading-edge, customer service–oriented company. These programs have been linked with the business imperatives and organizational capabilities needed to become the most successful airline in the business as well as to make BA a great place at which to work. The dual focus on making money and valuing employees has paid off.

Here are some of the processes, programs, and approaches that address these issues:

❑ A performance management system assesses the performance of all managers on a quarterly basis. The quarterly review does not have to be a formal, documented process, although a documented procedure is required annually. The system measures strengths and areas for personal development against a framework of management practices. Key areas of development are agreed upon and managers look to self-development programs to help them deliver top-level customer service.

❑ In supporting British Airways' quality strategy, "Winning for Customers" was the core program that gave managers an opportunity to further assess their skills and look for development areas.

❑ To support the messages of *Winners,* a series of programs for managers called "Managing Winners" was developed. These programs employed 360-degree feedback collected prior to the program to help individual managers identify their personal strengths and areas that called for further improvement.

❑ A selection of programs, beginning with a one-day meeting, introduced BA employees to the concept and practice of service recovery and the value to the business of customer retention. More than 40,000 employees attended such meetings during a 2-year period.

❑ The Quest Management Development Centre was launched to provide open learning facilities across British Airways. The learning center is dedicated to the management grades. Within the center there are sophisticated computer learning facilities, cassettes, self-paced programs, and other tools. All managers are currently completing compulsory health and safety programs through the open learning center.

Focus

The core strategy that pulled British Airways out of the also-ran category of international air carriers is its total dedication to the passenger.

All airlines talk about passenger service ("The Friendly Skies," "We love to fly," and so on), but few of them are dedicated to the passenger. In talking to airline pilots, one learns that often they are rewarded for fuel consumption more than for passenger comfort, on-time arrival, or even safety. Every frequent flyer has run across poorly trained, highly stressed personnel who cannot give the kind of service that the advertising department trumpets. At BA, everyone is totally focused on the comfort of the passenger. Passenger ratings consistently rank BA among the top two or three airlines for service and comfort.

The company practices long-term commitment to its core strategy by designing training programs with a ten-year outlook. This precludes jumping on every management fad that comes along. Strategic goals for the future have been identified, along with the plans, values, and cultural factors that management and staff have to attend to in achieving those goals. This has enabled BA to identify the capabilities it needs to deliver the strategy. In turn, this shapes BA's training and development approach to the future.

Training Expressly Supporting the Customer Strategy

British Airways' approach to training has been based on the customer's needs since its first corporate program, "Customer First," in 1985. This program reemphasized the importance of excellent service in achieving British Airways' vision of being "the best and most successful company in the airline business."

Training programs are part of an integrated system that builds on the key messages and learning of previous programs. This includes "Winning for Customers," which communicated not only the importance of continued excellent customer service but also the value of customer loyalty and retention. The program educated all employees on the benefits to the business of service recovery—what to do when service fails. They recognize that problems will happen and that systems and people will fail. Those who can recover quickly will be the winners in the increasingly competitive international air carrier market.

Leadership 2000 is the current example of focusing on a long-term core strategy. Because large-scale capital investment is fundamental to air transport, carriers must plan for the long haul. British Airways recognizes the importance of both leadership and organizational capacity for achieving the next ten-year business plan. The strategy requires enhanced management capability to further develop and sustain processes that enable people to deliver more effectively. These programs have been designed to link with the core strategy expressed in the Winning for Customers strategy. As British Airways begins to deliver on the requirements of Leadership 2000, it is reviewing, evaluating, and updating current programs, where appropriate, in line with the capability framework.

Turbulence

BA's transformation was not an easy task. Changing a 50,000-employee, multibillion-dollar capital base, worldwide operation is not an overnight job. A number of obstacles had to be overcome during the first few critical years. These were some typical problems and barriers:

❑ The global nature and size of British Airways made it difficult to process all managers and personnel through the programs.
❑ A number of the 1980s staff opposed change in the early days and didn't support the training initiatives. Not surprisingly, these people either chose to leave the company, or we helped to find an organization where they might feel more comfortable.
❑ Creative change was difficult to implement within the constraints of an extremely tight cost structure. The pressures of operating under the burden of a massive debt load limit one's actions.
❑ Trade unions were an obstacle in the early days. Fear of job loss as well as concern for the survival of the union's power functioned as a restraint.

Over time, the company has found that obstacles are best overcome by building support from within the culture. Management has been able to initiate changes and maintain momentum by:

❑ *"Sowing seeds"* around the organization by means of the supporters of change and the training initiatives.
❑ *Empowering the staff.* For example, management set up "Customer First" groups in the terminals. Initially, this led to diffi-

culties. The employees did not have clear guidelines as to how much discretion they could exercise with the customers. In the beginning, this meant inconsistent and arbitrary treatment. Upon reviewing the problem, the level of authority delegated to the employees was clarified. Once the people knew just how far they could go, the problem was solved.

❑ *Emphasizing and rewarding a philosophy of continual improvement that thrives on innovation.* Three BHAM factors— culture, risk, and never being satisfied—were integrated. Taking prudent risks in pursuit of continual improvement became a new cultural norm.

The British Airways Way of Managing Training

Training as a cohesive function linked to specific corporate initiatives and having its own departmental level goals is virtually unknown. Despite what some training professionals might argue, the evidence is that the training function is typically a conglomeration of loosely connected programs and courses. At the end of the day, it is very difficult for anyone to show that training has fulfilled a specific charter. BA is an exception to this rule. The training function has standards for good practice that are tied to the customer service imperative. The following standards are applied within the training and development process:

1. The management of the training function started with a mandate to build skills in customer service from every angle possible and practical.
2. They then ensure a consistent approach by providing a framework that supports the skills taught within the trainers' personal development modules.
3. Performance standards are set for trainers in the area of professional capability.
4. Customer service training practices are benchmarked both internally and externally as a means of finding the most cost-effective methods.
5. Line managers are partnered with trainers to work out a common understanding and a common language to ensure practical training methods and value-adding results from training.

British Airways has adopted this set of practices for managing the activity of the training and development function. By adhering to these criteria, it ensures that training provides a maximum return to the organization.

The first issue is to ensure that training activities are linked to business plans. Performance analysis establishes a need to change performance to improve customer service. Because each job is connected to customer service, it is easy to spot failure points. The question then is: Is training an appropriate and potentially useful course of action? If it appears to be, a skills analysis sets the aims of that training by establishing performance objectives and an assessment of the potential value of that performance to the business.

The corollary to the first point is to identify the best solutions—training and nontraining. Design of learning intervention focuses on the connection between given skill objectives and the most practical training methods. This ensures that the stated training/learning objectives are achieved in ways that are cost-effective, that maximize learning and skill building for individuals, and that facilitate transfer of the knowledge and skills to the workplace.

The training delivery method often uses both professional training staff and line personnel to enhance maximum learning. Personal needs are also considered so that a one-size-fits-all mentality does not diminish training effectiveness at the individual level.

Finally, a tangible value for the training investment is set before the training commences. This is a most extraordinary practice. Saratoga Institute's research over a ten-year period with 1,000 companies found that less than 10 percent set any type of ROI (return on investment) goal before the training is delivered. Likewise, less than 15 percent measure ROI after the fact. At British Airways, measures for the effectiveness of training as it occurs are taken and overall quantitative return on investment is calculated after the fact. This includes determining the extent to which the performance objectives have been met in the workplace and the expected return on the investment achieved.

Results

To date, British Airways has invested approximately £130 million per annum in the training of people. As a result, British Airways' customers have been treated to a marked improvement in customer service, and the organization has moved from losing £200 per minute to being the most profitable airline in the world. By shifting from being an operationally driven to a market/customer-dedicated airline, it has proved the efficacy of the BHAM approach. Dual values of people and profit, a long-term core strategy of customer service, a customer-focused culture, partnering with employees to change the culture, risk taking, and never being satisfied are all hallmarks of British Airways.

The approach to human development has not only had a positive impact on the organization's profitability, it has established British Airways as an airline dedicated to serving the customer. Training has been delivered to unvarying standards as a result of the training and development criteria followed by all training functions in BA. This uniform approach is a result of the training and development strategy steering group, which meets to discuss generic training issues that need to be handled consistently across the business.

The training and development function was chosen as the vehicle in this case because it exemplifies the British Airways mentality. The human development operation is a microcosm of the corporate approach to doing business. Clear goals, rigorous planning, in-depth analysis and assessment, proven standard methods, and measures of effectiveness ensure high levels of human asset management.

Case prepared by Richard Phelps, Managing Director, Saratoga Europe.

CANADIAN IMPERIAL BANK OF COMMERCE
TORONTO, ONTARIO

Background

Several years ago, the top executive group at CIBC (Canadian Imperial Bank of Commerce) took a look at the bank and decided it needed to steer a new course, under the leadership of Chairman & CEO Al Flood. At the time, CIBC was the number-two bank in asset size in Canada, behind the Royal Bank of Canada. Overall, the bank had been relatively successful, yet it ranked only fifth or sixth nationally on several financial indicators such as return on equity, shareholder value, and net income. Over the next five years, management began to remake the bank, and as of the second quarter of 1996, it was number one in return on equity.

Two forces drove the need for change: technology and customers. With the increasing investment in technology, banking processes changed. The introduction of ATMs and other new services not only opened up new opportunities, it demanded new ways of working. Historically, the bank grew by adding branches to gain market share. It opened the door and told the customers what it *could* do for them. However, in the 1990s, with customers becoming more knowledgeable and demanding, they started to tell the bank what it *should* do for them. As the market changed, management realized that the bank had to offer a more wholistic approach to financial services. Rather than a set of discrete services like checking accounts, savings accounts, and safe deposit boxes, the offering would have to be presented as an integrated package of services. With this change in service context came a need to develop the people to deliver it.

As was typical of most banking institutions, CIBC was a hierarchical structure. Everyone knew there was a prescribed way of doing everything. Managers gave people their assignments every morning and they were expected to perform accordingly—with new products, an integrated service model, and more demanding customers, that no longer worked. People had to be given some latitude, and managers had to shift from quoting rules to coaching performance. On paper, it sounded doable, but a 1990 employee survey revealed a problem. Most employees reported a lack of focus on and understanding of the strategy of the company. They felt little pride in their work, and also felt essentially bound up by the structure. In short, it was clear that an entire makeover was needed.

Human Systems

A major part of the makeover was in the human systems and processes. In 1990, CIBC had 48,000 employees—880 of whom were in the human resources function. That same year, Michele Darling, executive vice president of human resources, arrived. Five years later, the human asset management systems had been reengineered and restructured. Today, there are some 37,000 employees—with about 500 of them in HR.

All major components of human asset management were redesigned. The job classification system, which carried the burden of thirty-two layers, was scrapped in favor of a broad-band compensation structure. This gave managers more latitude in recognizing performance.

The performance management system had the typical high-end rating skew. Most systems tend to yield ratings that are inflated above the standard bell-shaped curve. This would have been acceptable if performance had matched it. The new system positions the supervisor as a performance coach. Jobs are defined around competencies and attributes. Performance objectives are set by the supervisor and employee. The employee develops a personal work-and-development plan, thereby linking job and career.

There had been no job-posting system. Progression depended on whom you knew as much as on what you knew. Some people resigned from one division of the company, only to show up later in another division as a new employee, after having enjoyed the severance benefits from the first job. Now there is a centralized database with control over job openings and separations.

Another major restructuring occurred in the training system. As with many organizations, training at CIBC was not managed. People were sent to training, but often this was not connected to their job, and not evaluated after the fact. Such a lax system had to end because the training investment was not delivering the knowledge that the chairman of CIBC knew was required for the new bank.

As Peter Drucker[1] has pointed out: In the new information economy knowledge is not just another resource, it is *the* most powerful resource. Knowledge is created by the interaction of people within an organization. Organizations are more than information processors, they *are* information and, even more important, they are knowledge creators. In the effective organization of the information economy, people are continually learning and reshaping their organizations.

To serve as the cornerstone of this knowledge creation machine, the chairman established the CIBC Leadership Centre north of Toronto, which would be the focal point of a systematic redeployment of employee development programs. A key element within that system was to be the leadership program. This was to help managers understand the changes that were taking place, the new core strategy that had been adopted, and their role. Senior executives would meet with managers, and exchange views on the changing organization. Mutual expectations would be discussed and shared. The training classes would be mixed by level and division to promote broader views and stimulate partnering. This would deemphasize hierarchies and draw attention to the value of cross-border teaming. In 1996, the chairman stated that a significant portion of the improvement in bank operations and performance could be attributed to this leadership program. The model for this new learning organization is presented below.

CIBC as a Learning Organization

The organizations of the past hundred years were formed to operate in the relatively stable and predictable environment of the industrial marketplace. As a result, the current speed of organizational renewal is too slow to cope with the velocity of change brought to the marketplace by the knowledge era. In *Human Value Management,*[2] I described this by stating that we are facing evolutionary changes coming at revolutionary speed.

In the thirty-five years between 1960 and 1995, 370, or more than 65 percent, of the Fortune 500 firms disappeared. Faced with the speed and power of these inexorable forces of change, CIBC's management asked, "How do we make sure that our organization is on track for long-term sustainability?" The answer was that they had to create an organization that could learn at least as fast as the market could change.

For CIBC, organizational learning is the conscious and systematic acquisition of the capabilities required to realize business strategies. There must be:

❑ Focus—a clear sense of destination
❑ Capability—skills and knowledge, processes and resources
❑ Commitment—attitudes, emotions, will, and ownership

The key strategic advantage of the third millennium will lie in consciously and intentionally improving the organization's capacity to learn faster and better than its competitors can. This will give the bank the capability to respond quickly, exploit emerging markets, generate new ideas, create new value-adding business processes, enhance the level of service, and accelerate organizational change.

The Learning Organization Model

Figure 10-1 is CIBC's conceptualization of the learning organization. The bank has divided its learning into four levels: individual, team, organizational, and customer. The learning organization concept operates under two principles: The individual is at the center of all learning, and each of the levels acts as a foundation for the next level.

Individual Learning

On this level, employees are encouraged to learn continuously, and are rewarded for their increasing competence. Learning does not take place in a vacuum. The imperative for individual learning is to move from a culture of entitlement to one in which individuals exercise personal responsibility for learning and career development. It starts with a recruitment strategy that selects people with the appropriate attri-

Figure 10-1. CIBC learning model.

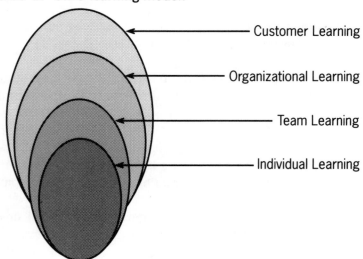

Customer Learning

Organizational Learning

Team Learning

Individual Learning

butes and competency potential. CIBC puts in place a learning system that has four phases in which the individual:

1. Builds a competency map based on perceived opportunities and interests.
2. Assesses own competencies on the basis of feedback from actions taken.
3. Formulates a personal developmental plan founded on future requirements and current competencies.
4. Acquires competence through practice, takes stock, and modifies the competency map, starting the cycle over again.

Team Learning

In a team environment, people share assumptions, learn through dialogue, build new mind-sets, and actively transfer their learning to others. The precursor to team learning is a collective agenda and a jointly owned business plan. The most important aspect of this type of learning is the formation of more effective mind-sets. This takes place as people are taught how to observe data, identify patterns and relationships among the data, build a mental map, and finally design new maps that move the organization forward.

Organizational Learning

This occurs when the organization builds the capability to regularly create new market opportunities and to quickly capitalize on the pursuit of a common purpose. The prerequisite to this is the management of interdependencies throughout the organization. The organization, through its people, must develop the capability to apply strategy, systems, structure, and culture for continuous improvement. Strategy includes the goals of the organization and how it seeks to serve them. Systems are the way that information and products/services flow through the organization. Structure defines the relationship between organizational members. Culture is the sum of opinions, shared mindsets, values, and norms.

Like BHAM companies everywhere, CIBC recognized that culture must be managed. Hubert Saint-Onge, the architect of the Leadership Centre's program, put it well:

Organizational culture is an often neglected dimension of organizational capability because it is largely operating at an implicit level. And yet, the organizational culture becomes even more important in knowledge-intensive organizations where a significant part of the organization is in people's minds.

He goes on to describe how culture is an integral element of organizational capability. It must be strong and cohesive to allow for the effective management of interdependencies. It must be tied to the strategic intent and business strategies of the organization. And it must be flexible enough to meet the requirements of the business.

To the organizational learning segment, CIBC added a simple and obvious but nonetheless brilliant tag. Organizational capability is greatest when every individual assumes leadership responsibility. No one waits to be told what to do or how to do it. The learning ethic instills the requirement that every person take responsibility for him- or herself, as well as for driving the organization forward. Titles and positions are less important than are knowledge and skill.

Customer Learning

This is the final element in CIBC's learning model. Here again the bank has gone beyond most organizational learning models to integrate the all-important customer. Customer learning takes place when the ultimate product is the learning of the customer. By involving the bank's customers through feedback mechanisms, the company is able to learn what the customer wants, while the customer learns how to use bank services more cost-effectively. This mutual learning builds an unparalleled level of customer loyalty. CIBC's notion of customer learning is built on the statement of John Seely Brown, corporate vice president of Xerox PARC, who claims that: "At some point in the not-too-distant future, some companies might not sell products, but rather the expertise to help users define their needs and create the products best suited to them. The company's product will be its customers' learning."

The BHAM Connection

Throughout the unfolding of the CIBC makeover, you can see the BHAM factors at work.

❑ *Value focus.* Inherent in the entire model and in the management philosophy that underpins it is the notion that the bank must serve employees, customers, and shareholders. It will not build long-term sustainability with a short-term profits-first approach.

❑ *Core strategy.* CIBC has not only talked about investing heavily in constructing an enduring enterprise. The goal is to design and perpetuate an institution that responds quickly, generates new value-adding structures and processes, encourages consistent service and quality, and accelerates change. This is the vocabulary of institution builders.

❑ *Culture.* Culture is a cornerstone of organizational learning at CIBC. It is part of the foreground—an integral element in the company's capability. There is an explicit statement of linkage with the company's strategic intent and business strategy. Even among BHAM companies, we have seldom seen culture so explicitly a part of the organization's management philosophy and systems.

❑ *Partnering and collaboration.* CIBC openly recognizes another BHAM factor by preaching collaboration both within and across business units. It is the stated precursor to organizational-level learning. In operation, it means the adoption of a collective agenda, shared visions, and the congruence of cultural and structural processes. When you have this confluence of processes as a value, you are naturally promoting partnering because the one can't exist without the other. One of the principles of the CIBC model is that there must be shared responsibilities to take advantage of the interdependence and to collaborate across functional boundaries.

❑ *Innovation and risk.* Attempting to learn faster and better than the competition does is the driver behind the Leadership Centre investment. CEO Flood took a big personal risk with his restructuring of the bank and its multimillion-dollar investment in training. He knew it was the logical, essential thing to do. CIBC aims to be the premier bank of Canada. Its people could carry it to this position if the bank's management takes the risk of funding this very innovative approach to learning.

❑ *Competitive passion.* The notion of a continuous, evolving state of change and growth is part of CIBC's basic insight into what the knowledge era requires. The bank points out that in the industrial era, incremental changes linked fixed states. In the knowledge game, improvement is the basic currency.

CIGATAM (CIGARROS LA TABACALERA MEXICANA)
MEXICO CITY

Cigatam was founded in 1898 in Mexico City and currently operates a total of three manufacturing plants and one tobacco processing plant. Total employment is 3,428. It produces several lines of tobacco products and is part of one of the most important Mexican business groups, Grupo Carso. Philip Morris owns 29 percent of the stock. In 1980, Cigatam had nearly 28 percent of the national market; by 1995, it enjoyed 48 percent of it.

Continuous Improvement

In 1982, Cigatam began its dedication to continuous improvement by starting in the production department. It was rewarded with consistently positive results. In 1985, the human resources department took the leadership in promoting this process in the service areas. Management felt that HR was the natural place from which to drive this companywide effort because the first step was to obtain the support of the work force.

From the beginning of the improvement program there was a strong emphasis on performance measurement. This followed the widely held belief that "you can't improve what you don't measure." The HR staff, motivated by the early success of the continuous improvement program, wanted to develop an objective measurement system and to this end engaged Saratoga Institute Mexico to lead them in the design of human performance measures. In May 1995 they produced their first set of metrics, which they presented at the Continuous Improvement Process meeting, a semiannual affair attended by the CEO and the directors of the company. The display showed data from the previous three years. This gave them a strong trend line with which to demonstrate the effects of their work.

Statistics and hard data are not a typical feature in either the Mexican culture or the culture of Cigatam. As one person put it, "The norteamericanos like to go to a game and know the statistics of the players and the teams. We like to go to the stadium, buy a cerveza, and just enjoy the game with our friends."

It was also contrary to the culture for staff departments to take the risk of showing the effects of their work. And here was the HR staff showing forty-four measures and threatening to find more. The line departments were startled and not necessarily happy. For the first time, HR was not speaking in terms of "mucho mas." Instead, it had numbers to provide a degree of precision and an objective view. Staff members displayed a strong sense of confidence and security based on knowing precisely what was happening. With their metrics the HR staff demonstrated how they were becoming a value-adding partner in the business.

The metrics showed where there had been performance improvements. Sometimes these improvements were of such a magnitude that it was clear that the process was then overstaffed. This allowed a reallocation of resources to areas needing improvement or to issues that were more critical or that offered greater opportunities. In effect, the metrics showed top management that the company could grow in sales and productivity without a parallel growth in staff support expenses.

The immediate reaction of the CEO and the directors was very positive. The CEO charged the other staff groups with developing their own metrics system. He wanted to learn the level of contribution from the functions that everyone had previously viewed as only expense centers. Within the next two years, the officers of the corporation were able to manage staff departments with a view toward realizing tangible value from them. In 1996, the metrics became part of the performance appraisal system. In the best BHAM tradition, the employees are involved in designing their own metric systems.

A Staffing Example

The objective of the staffing function is to obtain the best fit at the lowest cost and in the shortest possible time. Through participation in U.S. and Mexican HR financial surveys, Cigatam demonstrated that the time it took to fill jobs (from date of job opening until job offer is accepted) was lower than the industry average. It was able to illustrate progressive improvement in terms not only of time but also in terms of the cost of hire and quality of candidates. Figure 10-2 compares Cigatam's times, after its process improvement, with mean times for Mexico and the United States.

HR reduced the use of costly recruitment practices by benchmarking other North American practices. They found that the use of a variety of sources, such as professional association meetings, career fairs, networking with other recruiters, and universities, cut their reliance on more expensive sources. They also found that maintaining an accurate, timely, and complete databank on candidates helped them reduce the time needed to fill jobs. They have expanded their sources to about 100 companies that share candidate information. For this information they pay about $600 annually compared to about $500 for a single newspaper advertisement. In a three-year period, their revised recruitment strategy and tactics cut their hiring expenses by 13.4 percent.

The Quality Side

It doesn't make much sense or add any value if you cut costs at the expense of quality. Saving even $10,000 per hire would not make up for the damage caused by one bad hire in a critical position. BHAM companies typically analyze all sides of the issue before they put new programs in place. This is a primary reason that they are the Best. They take the time to fully understand the problem, its source, and the best solution to it. Conversely, our research has consistently come across staff departments that have no knowledge whatsoever of their operating costs other than their annual budget.

Early on in its improvement program, Cigatam introduced a com-

Figure 10-2. Number of days needed to fill and start jobs at Cigatam compared with Mexico and U.S.A.

1995	Cigatam	Mexico Mean	USA Mean
		(Days)	
Time to Fill	5	21	46
Time to Start	13	26	54

puter-based applicant tracking system. HR used it for more than record keeping and record retrieval. By carefully matching candidates with positions and looking beyond the obvious to the issue of "fit," it has been able to generate lists of highly qualified personnel. One test of quality is how well the person meets the job specs. The other is how well he or she fits in and performs after hiring. Cigatam's turnover rate was only 4 percent for the latest year tracked.

Before implementing the computerized system, Cigatam needed three persons and three hours daily to locate the résumés or applications of candidates who were available to fill vacant positions. Considering that they receive and have to cull approximately 5,000 applications a year to fill about 100 jobs, it meant a lot of work and a lot of staff time (and cost) devoted to paperwork. With the computer program, it takes only one person and three minutes to extract suitable candidates from the database. This is a reduction in daily processing time from nine hours to three minutes.

Handling the Unexpected

In 1995, Cigatam increased its temporary work force to support the rollout of a new product. This meant that HR had to cut its processing time for new hires. The standard time to run reference checks had been ten days, and the suppliers of drug screening took eight days to deliver test results. This was not acceptable in the new environment. Through negotiation and process improvement, Cigatam and the vendors were able to reduce their delivery times to six and four days respectively. These represented reductions of 40 percent in reference checking and 50 percent in drug screening.

The hiring process was also changed to a more direct method. Now hiring is a one-on-one conversation between recruiter and hiring manager. By putting the recruiters in close contact with their customers some of the paperwork has been eliminated. There are also dedicated staff members supporting various personnel functions for line departments. One example is the personal contribution analysis, now a part of the performance appraisal system. Employees can be tested for growth-potential assignments. They are directly informed and guided in the continuous improvement process. In short, there is now a much closer working partnership between line and staff. And it has paid off in both qualitative (service and quality) and quantitative (pro-ductivity) terms.

Conclusion

Through its continuous improvement and partnering policies, Cigatam has simplified its processes, decreased the time it takes to fill jobs, lowered its cost per hire, located high-quality candidates, cut operating expenses, and assisted management in sustaining a higher-than-stan-dard productivity. Through automation the human resources staff has positioned itself as an internal consultant rather than as a transaction processor.

All this has helped shift the culture from a loose system to one that, with hard data, can compete in the increasingly competitive world markets. Partnering is at the heart of the new approach, with line and staff working more closely together. Innovation and risk are now, for the first time, part of the culture. Central to its long-term con-tinuous improvement process is Cigatam's next step: It is preparing to launch a global benchmarking program. The company will seek out world-class enterprises anywhere from which it can learn and improve. All these changes have helped support the never-being-satisfied atti-tude so characteristic of a BHAM company.

Case prepared by the staff of Saratoga Institute Mexico under the direction of Managing Director Alfonso Gonzales Montesinas.

GRIFFINS FOODS LIMITED
AUCKLAND, NEW ZEALAND

Griffins Foods is a manufacturer of biscuits, crackers, savory snacks, and salad dressings. It is the second-largest branded packaged con-sumer food company in New Zealand and employs approximately 900 people at four sites. The company is wholly owned by Danone Group of France. Revenues exceeded NZ$230 (US$159) million in 1996. In 1990, it began a broad-based program to improve the way it recruited, prepared, managed, and recognized its employees. Ross Anderson, human resources director, described the strategy and tactics employed by Griffins to give the company a competitive advantage in the highly competitive consumer foods market.

Values and Core Strategy

One of the more noticeable features of the company is that it is very focused on the human as well as the financial side of its business. This covers employees, the community, and the union. Its values and strategy are consistent with those of other BHAM companies in being not only stated but also lived. Griffins has in place what it calls the Dual Project. The defining statement is as follows: "Griffins Foods will maintain a position of strength capable of performing well to the satisfaction of two essential groups—the employees and the shareholders. This is referred to as the Dual Economic and Social Project and is the centre of our human resources strategy."

An audit by the Auckland Employers Association confirmed that the Dual Project does indeed govern everything the company does. It is generally regarded internally as the key to Griffins' success and survival. Managing Director Frank Palantoni sums up the Dual Project:

> As the company succeeds, people should succeed. We therefore share that which creates success for the company and employees and eliminates competition between management and employees. It provides common goals and common rewards. Conflict precludes mutual benefit, so we are gradually changing the culture and attitudes of the organisation to one where everyone is on the same team. Previously, there was a lot of "them and us" type feeling.

The Dual Project led to the establishment of the Towards 2000 consultative committee and self-managing teams. It does not give away control of the business, but it does provide an honest opportunity for everyone to express their views. Management undertakes to "foster job enrichment for the well-being of our employees." This has been done by eliminating nonproductive and nonvalue-adding tasks and making work as interesting and challenging as possible. As a result, morale, skill levels, communications, and competitiveness have all improved. The money spent on these projects has already been recouped.

Today, the culture has evolved to the point where the Towards 2000 committees are no longer necessary. Now, joint consultation happens naturally on a day-to-day, informal basis.

In addition to their effect on the internal governance of the workplace, Dual Project values and core strategy influence the way in which Griffins interacts with the wider community. It means that the company takes economic actions that have social spin-offs. For example, it fosters employment growth in the areas in which the company operates. This gives Griffins a wider and more highly skilled prospective work force and leverages its subsequent actions.

Culture

Griffins understands that culture is a multidimensional force. It covers not only norms but also values, skills, and practices. Recruitment screens for core behaviors the company values because Griffiins' belief is that it is easier to teach skills than to change attitudes. The core behaviors are individual accountability, customer-driven activity, flexibility, teamwork, communications, and proactiveness, For supervisory positions, leadership is an additional requirement. Griffins moves people laterally as much as possible so that they can learn a broad range of skills and see things from different perspectives. Lateral moves also spread cultural norms.

The company is opening a Learning Network as a step towards becoming a learning organization. All books, articles, and internal and external course materials have been catalogued. Managers are registered on the network as coaches or facilitators in their areas of expertise. Personal learning is further supported through a 360-degree feedback system among the salaried population. The culture norm now is, "Feedback is the Breakfast of Champions."

A critically important aspect of any culture is its recognition system. The Griffins culture is definitely one of reward and recognition based on performance. An employee's position in the company is not necessarily determinant of his or her responsibility. For example, a secretary was put in charge of upgrading a computer system. Others have taken on responsibility for controlling capital expenditures, leasing fleet vehicles, and managing employee communications from the head office. When the company is making capital improvements, staff members are invited to have input in the design so that their jobs will be made easier and more personally rewarding as well as more efficient. There is also a practice of inviting relatively junior staff—the ones involved in the work processes—to meetings at which process changes are considered. Management's belief is that their people know what is actually happening, what the problems are, and probably what some of the solutions might be.

"Each manager is responsible for making human resource management a living thing," according to Griffins' managing director. The human resources department is charged with "delivering a competitive edge" by adding value to the human assets of the company. In operational terms, this means that HR aims at generating a sustainable, competitive advantage through people by developing effective communications, appropriate skills, and effective work organizations. To do this, the HR function has to interact and partner with line management, devolving many of its traditional tasks so that it can focus on the leveraging of human skills. The other side of this idea is that managers have to be trained to back responsibility for hiring, maintaining, and developing their human assets.

Two-Way Communications

When you attempt to empower people, you have to communicate. Griffins has made heroic efforts to communicate effectively in all directions. Some of its downward communication vehicles are shown in Figure 10-3.

There is an equal concern with upward communications. Griffins has long had an open door policy, but that is not enough. People have to feel confident that when they do walk through the door at Griffins, it will be worthwhile as well as safe. There are formal methods such as team meetings. But the proof of the effectiveness of the open door policy can be judged from the statement of a junior staff member, who commented, "You can just go in and say what you want to."

Underpinning these methods and practices is a strategy for each founded on the company's commitment to communicate at every opportunity its goals, its progress toward the goals, and the importance of its four key externals: customers, consumers, suppliers, and competitors.

Figure 10-3. Communication methods used by Griffins Foods.

Notice boards	Daily production charts
Newsletters	Customer complaint boards
Team meetings/10-minute talks	Crisis meetings for quality and start-up
Memoranda	Support and challenge teams
Face-to-face communications by managers on site	News flashes

As most BHAM companies have found, you can never communicate too much. As part of its communications skills effort, the company put its top seventy people through a listening skills and communication course. Griffins constantly monitors its communications system through surveys of employees' viewpoints. Although management has generally received high marks, it was criticized for not communicating the results of some employee surveys. The Auckland Employers Association audit rated Griffins' communications program at about 8 on a scale of 10. This rating compares favorably with that of most employers but still leaves room for improvement.

Partnering

One of the more significant examples of partnering—and one with some potential risk—is the company's work with the unions. The Dual Project calls for employees to be well represented, and Griffins encourages and supports strong union representation. This is very unusual in an industry and a country not noted for sanguine management/labor relations. In New Zealand, most employers are trying to minimize union involvement in favor of dealing directly with employees. Griffins has taken a more positive track. It even supported a trip to Europe for some union personnel, and provided an opportunity for them to meet with union officials there. The openness and support gained the company a lot of trust from the unions. Union representatives at Griffins have access to many meetings and activities within the company. The payoffs have been smoother operations for the company and a reduction of surprises at contract time. Contract negotiations now go smoothly because of the improved level of communications.

Partnering with employees also takes place when employees are involved in system design projects and communications meetings. Partnering also implies involving people from across different functions to get a job done.

Summary

Griffins has achieved an enviable financial record, in no small part owing to the values and methods that have informed its human asset management effort. Since beginning its reforms in performance management in 1990, sales volume per employee has increased by over 60 percent. A profit sharing scheme, covering the entire Griffins team, has been in place since 1993. This is another case that demonstrates unequivocally the connection between human asset management and financial accomplishment.

Case prepared by Robyn McKinney, Auckland Employers Association, and Ross Andersen, Griffins Foods Ltd.

PEQUIVEN
CARACAS, VENEZUELA

Background

The petrochemical industry is a highly competitive sector within the global market, now undergoing deep changes affecting the structure and performance of companies within the industry. The Venezuelan petrochemical industry is the leading source of foreign exchange for the country. Pequiven is one of the companies within Petroleos de Venezuela (PDVSA), the leading oil company commissioned by the state to ensure the economic development of the national petroleum industry as a whole. Pequiven has operations in three states, and is headquartered in the capital, Caracas.

Pequiven produces a broad range of petrochemicals, fertilizers, resins, plastics, and related natural gas derivatives for the domestic and international markets. Of its production, 34 percent is exported, principally to the United States, Colombia, and Chile. In 1995, it had sales of $775,000,000. As of May 1996, the company employed 4,171 persons.

Transformation

Following an economic crisis early in the 1990s, Pequiven began a deep transformation in both its administrative and operating areas. Part of the reason for this transformation effort was to prepare the company for privatization. Top management has established concrete objectives to ensure that the transformation reach all of the company including administrative services. By mid 1996, this program began to effect a financial turnaround. It continues to drive a steady growth in income and profits.

One key objective was to turn staff functions such as human resources into value-adding operations. The transformation project shows some of the process, with emphasis on two elements:

1. The entrepreneurial or business framework in which the transformation of the human asset managing function (human resources) took place
2. The transformation process itself

The BHAM factors were specifically applied with an eye toward adding value and establishing a solid foundation for future growth. In operation, it became clear that the factors could be used as practical design criteria transportable across departments.

The Process

The process to transform Pequiven was led by Arnold Volkenborm, chairman of the board, and Francisco Camargo, director of human resources, and associates Maria de Rodriguez and Luis Pulgar.

Strategic Business Objectives

Pequiven set five strategic objectives:

1. 5 percent increase in its gross production, year to year
2. 16 percent increase in sales
3. reduction of the gross industrial accident rate
4. net gain in profit to 59 billion bolivars
5. Obtaining the ISO 9002 certificate for polyvinyl chloride and nitrogen plants at Moron, and accreditation by the *Guide 180 25* for the Zulia Complex laboratory site

The Human Asset Side

As part of the transformation, the human resources function pledged to achieve the following human asset management objectives:

❑ Establishing a performance evaluation system that measures value-added and continuous improvement using internal performance data and comparing it to outside benchmarks.
❑ Focusing on operational efficiency indexes, cost reduction, and key competence development.
❑ Fostering a service culture throughout the company.
❑ Promoting employee communications, teamwork, and improvements in supervision.
❑ Generating creative solutions to improving quality of life standards in the workplace and at home.

Pequiven maintains human resources offices in Caracas and at the three operating sites. The ratio of HR staff to employees by location is shown in Figure 10-4.

HR expense as a percentage of total Pequiven expenses is 3.57 percent. This is high by international standards. However, in Pequiven and the other petroleum subsidiaries of PDVSA, the HR function also manages many social and educational community activities that are not covered by human resources departments in other countries. This includes managing schools, hospitals and clinics, and recreational facilities.

Figure 10-4. Ratio of HR staff to employees in four locations.

Location	HR	Employees	Ratio
Corporate offices	46	556	1:12
El Tablazo	49	2,293	1:48
Moron	44	1,078	1:25
Jose	12	259	1:21

Planning

A performance measurement system was designed by human resources, under the sponsorship of the board of directors, to stimulate an increase in productivity. It was installed in the following departments: administration and services, computation, corporate affairs, legal affairs, medical services, and public affairs. This is a key part of the transformation program. In this case, the purpose of the measures was to monitor and improve performance to the tune of $50 million in the corporate offices in 1996.

Production and Finance Applications

The PSM program was installed in production, where it was aimed at improving productivity 5 to 7 percent in the manufacturing areas. Specifically, objectives were set to increase production volume, improve safety, provide environmental protection, enhance product quality, reduce overtime, etc. An example of the effects of focusing on the human asset side of the business was that in a typical quarter in early 1996, there were improvements in production, environmental indexes, safety, and quality, which contributed several million dollars to the bottom line.

In finance, a training program was designed and carried out to improve skills in budget preparation. This focused primarily on manpower budgeting, including the development and monitoring of critical ratios and accounts that affect the financial position of the company.

The process is now in operation, and it shows early signs of meeting the goal of yielding savings in the millions.

Venezuela's pay regulations are very complicated. Administration is costly and susceptible to errors. As one of the process improvement programs, they set out new procedures and new measures to monitor progress in improving payroll administration. The monitoring ratios helped identify sources of efforts. In the first three months, more than $30,000 was saved.

A computerized system was introduced into human resources. It tracked operating goals for every program and process. Each goal is set to measure two values. One is the amount of change as expressed in percentages (i.e., time and volume improvements). The other is the impact of the change expressed in monetary terms. This second measure, impact, is unusual for many human resources functions, which seldom find ways to express the economic value of their work.

Conclusion

According to the Pequiven management, "Everyone is looking at the value that their goals are adding to the business." This value focus is seen when staff programs are proposed. Now they are directly linked to corporate objectives and carry an estimate of how the new schemes will generate economic value and contribute to the corporate treasury. Each goal has expected percentage increases and monetary values. The computerized performance measurement system gives everyone feedback on a regular basis. Today, all managers can express their program results in money, time, volume, or quality terms. This transformation process, founded on BHAM principles, driven by a value orientation and supported by modern computer technology, is repositioning Pequiven for a successful shift to privatization.

Case prepared by Jose Kutos and Eleo Ventocilla of DKV Associados (Saratoga Institute, Venezuela).

QUEENSLAND TREASURY
BRISBANE, AUSTRALIA

Queensland is Australia's sunshine state. Located on the northeast coast, it has been growing rapidly as a favored resort center. This growth has put a significant strain on governmental services. The Queensland Treasury provides financial and economic advice to the state government with the aim of enhancing the state's financial position and economic performance. It also has responsibility for the Office of Women's Affairs and the Office of Arts and Cultural Development. Queensland Treasury employs approximately 1,250 staff members, who are mainly based in the state's capital, Brisbane.

The management group of Queensland Treasury felt a need to improve efficiency in an era of increasing public criticism of governmental waste. The human resources department was chosen as a starting point and as an example of how a traditional expense center can be monitored and managed for the purpose of increasing efficiency and adding value rather than expense.

The Treasury began the process by gathering data and reporting on the costs of providing human resource services. This was accomplished by accurately tracking HR staff members' time allocation and adding this to capital and accommodation costs. The system generates benefits at a number of levels:

- ❑ It allows the HR department to effectively cost its services.
- ❑ It improves the capacity for strategic management, enabling analysis of whether investment in HR is being made in value-adding services or in make-work activities.
- ❑ It improves operational management, enabling analysis of workload peaks and troughs for optimum efficiency.
- ❑ It assists in resource allocation at both strategic and operational levels.
- ❑ It increases staff awareness of how time allocation is contributing to the achievement of the department's objectives.
- ❑ It highlights areas needing attention.

Figure 10-5 shows the process flow within the department.

Need for the Practice

The purpose of this scheme is not to spy on people or to make sure that they are working hard all day. Time-recording systems have been around since at least the beginning of the Industrial Revolution. Em-

Figure 10-5. Flowchart of the time allocation process within HR.

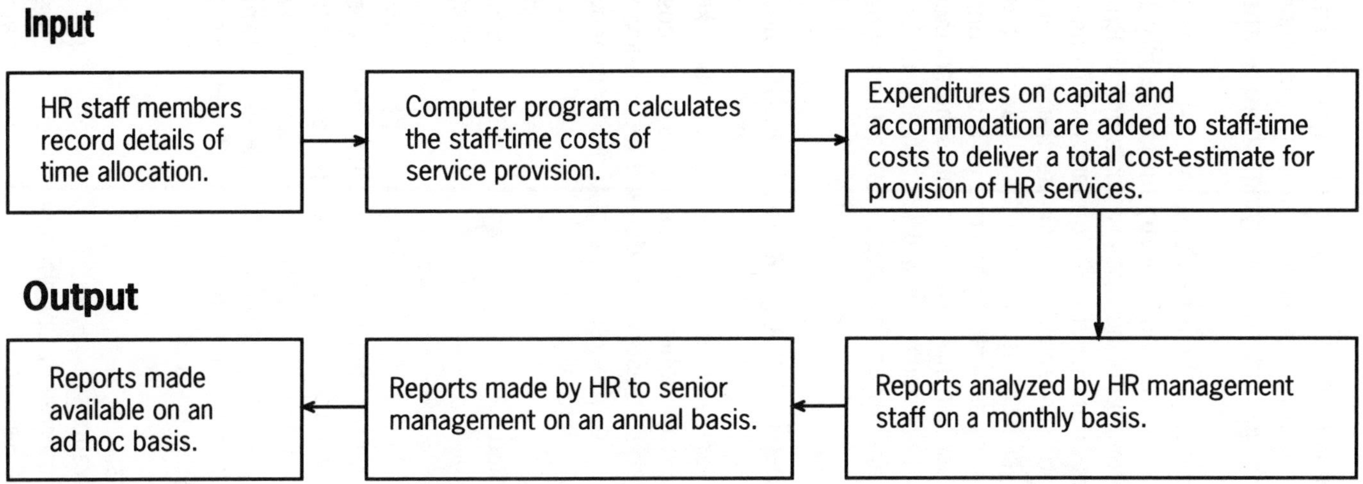

Input

Output

ployees have learned how to beat any system. The objective in this case was to improve operations, simplify processes, make jobs less boring, and reduce costs by studying where each person's time was being spent.

In the provision of HR services, the major cost component is salaries. But most analyses of investment in the HR department do not allow for delineation of how salary costs are allocated to various services. It is important for the HR department to target its resources in the direction of services that facilitate the achievement of organizational objectives. It is also important for the HR department, and other staff departments as well, to be seen as a value-adding service rather than as an expense center. By using this scheme, the department management can also monitor how it is spending its budget and chart its expenditures against achievement of objectives.

The Time Allocation Practice at Work

At the end of each working day, HR staff members key into a computer program (called Microtime) the details of how they have spent their day. Queensland Treasury has devised a three-level scheme to facilitate the quick, reliable recording of time allocation. The three levels, from macro to micro, are:

❑ Function
❑ Category
❑ Task

For example, for the recruitment function, a category might be Advertising, and a task might be Dispatch position description. Staff members record their time allocation at the task level in terms of the number of hours spent at each task. The sample table in Figure 10-6 shows categories and tasks for recruitment. The other functions used in Queensland Treasury's scheme are:

ABC Consulting
Administration
Equal Employment Opportunity
Employee Relations

Figure 10-6. Example of scheme as applied to recruitment function.

Function	Category	Task
Recruitment	Advertising	Advertising/enter on Aptrack
		Dispatch position description
	Résumé collection	Register applications
		Collate and forward to chair
	Interview procedure	Arrange interview panel
		Finalize recruitment
		Interview panel member
	Appeals	Appeals documentation
	Advice	Appeals advice
		Recruitment advice/inquiries
	Invoice preparation	Invoice preparation for payment
	Recruitment administration	Recruitment processing
	Traineeship administration	Training processing

Job Evaluations
Payroll
Policy Development
Scholarship Program
Establishment
Graduate Recruitment/Vacation Employment
Special Projects

This scheme is tailored to different classification levels. The smallest unit of analysis is a quarter of an hour. If staff spent all day writing a policy (that is, on one discrete task) they would simply record spending eight hours on that task. This process of time reporting takes no more than five minutes at the end of each day. Before this system was inaugurated, staff signed "time sheets." So they were accustomed to making daily reports regarding their time. The former system, however, was not used to any strategic or administrative advantage.

Time is recorded in terms of the actual number of hours spent rather than as a percentage of each day's activities. This is done for several reasons. First, it allows HR management to monitor any level of unpaid overtime. If staff members are regularly undertaking significant amounts of unpaid overtime, this would show up. It should be investigated because in the long term, staff accuracy, productivity, and morale may decrease and turnover increase as a result. Second, records are kept in terms of the actual number of hours so that external clients may be charged appropriately.

Microtime maintains salary details for each staff member and calculates the staff time cost of providing each service. The next step is the calculation of HR's total expenditures on capital and accommodation.

Development of the Scheme

The methodology was developed within the HR department with the help of an external consultant, whose fees were about $25,000 to $30,000. All HR staff members were involved in the development of the scheme, as was the HR director's manager. The HR director's manager was very supportive of the scheme, especially as it was focused on and would result in real data that could be used to improve operational performance.

Once the practice proved to be administratively simple, acceptable to employees, and useful for management, it was extended to all departments within Queensland Treasury's Corporate Services Division. The HR department provided a consultancy service to facilitate the scheme's modification for and implementation in individual work units.

Development costs included the external consultant's fee as well as HR staff members' time. The cost of the computer software was negligible. At the end of each month, data administration costs about one day's worth of an operative's salary. The cost in staff time of actually making the daily report is considered to be negligible, especially in that it replaces an existing time reporting procedure that was used to no strategic advantage.

BHAM Application

It doesn't take a great deal of effort to find evidence of the BHAM factors in this focused example.

Value Focus

As in all BHAM situations, the organizational values and culture work together with the operating and administrative systems. Queensland Treasury's corporate values are:

❑ Leadership—providing citizens with a good return on their tax support
❑ Results—fostering an environment of achievement
❑ Teamwork—for the benefit of all
❑ Service—to both citizens and employees

Treasury management sees this practice as integral to the ethic of always seeking value. The practice balances human and financial values in that management is able to program objectives on the basis of the real costs of doing business. Management is able to monitor and reward the efforts made by staff members. Staff job satisfaction is increased when members are able to see how their individual efforts are contributing to the achievement of departmental objectives.

Strategic Commitment

This practice supports the corporate services group's basic goal of improving the long-term strategic and operational performance of the Treasury portfolio. At the outset, the HR director considered it important to gain both senior management support and employee support for the introduction of the practice. Commitment to the practice became much easier once HR managers demonstrated their effective use of the information, and thus of the resources of the department, to both senior managers and staff.

Culture

Because of the nature of its business, the culture of Queensland Treasury is focused on money. This practice fits in with that culture, demonstrating that the department can maximize its value without increasing costs. A cultural value of fiscal management is linked with a system of managing staff time, the basis of cost management. By applying the practice, the Treasury can use valid, objective data to assist a decision to transfer resources from process-focused activities to more strategic objectives.

Partnering

Initially, the HR department demonstrated the advantages of this practice. Later, it assisted in implementing the practice throughout the Treasury's Corporate Services Division. One standard method helps senior management compare apples with apples in the planning and allocation of resources.

Collaboration

All HR functions were involved in the design as well as the implementation of the practice.

Communication

Initially, there was some resistance to the practice because of its perceived links with a "big brother" style of management. However, the extensive and detailed briefing sessions that accompanied the design and implementation of the practice helped make staff very comfortable with the practice.

Innovation and Risk

There were fears that staff members would not embrace this new way of managing resources. Some in management were concerned that the staff might rebel or engage in some form of work slowdown or stoppage. Few people like to have their time closely monitored. But a program of open and extensive communications explained why the Treasury had to do this as a means of cost control.

Competitive Passion

Feedback on the practice is encouraged during the department's regular staff meetings. The methodology initially developed has already been refined. Planned improvements include using activity-based costing to attain quality assurance accreditation. After the department's information system has been updated, it will use activity-based costing to assist with a major reengineering program.

Summary

Queensland Treasury's adoption of a new time allocation procedure allows analysis of how a major investment—staff time—is allocated across a wide range of strategic and operational activities. Staff services are usually included in corporate costs rather than costed separately. Clearly, the practice is applicable to organizations within the public sector, as well as to many others in private industry where there is no cultural conflict.

Since the introduction of the practice, the HR department has demonstrated that it has been more productive in achieving specific objectives relative to industrial relations and enterprise bargaining. Overall operating costs have not been reduced, but they have been deployed to more strategic, value-adding areas. One example of a specific cost reduction is recruitment. Between 1994 and 1995 the Treasury's recruitment cost factor (average cost of hiring employees) dropped from $A4,399 to $A1,253. This is a 71 percent reduction. It places Queensland Treasury among the best 25th percentile in the Saratoga Australian Human Resource Effectiveness Report organizations.

In addition to direct cost reductions, the HR department expects to see a reduction in the number of employee grievances. More time is now being devoted to employee relations as opposed to administrative activity.

The proof of the effectiveness of the time allocation practice is obvious. It would not have been extended across the entire Corporate Services Division if it had not proven effective in human resources. Effectiveness is measurable at three levels: cost management, service improvement (value added), and employee satisfaction. Queensland Treasury achieved all three values through adopting this system.

Case prepared by Peter Howes and the staff of HRM Consulting, Brisbane (Saratoga Australia).

Conclusion

There is sufficient evidence to support the conclusion that best practices in human management are universal. They vary only according to local conditions. Managers would be safe in employing them in any industrialized or emerging industrial economy so long as they are sensitive to the unique forces at play in any particular locale. Culture, economics, laws and regulations, the state of technology, and other national or regional forces affect the operation of any organization. But the basics endure.

References

1. Peter F. Drucker, *Managing in a Time of Great Change* (New York: Dutton, 1995), pp. 165–170.
2. Jac Fitz-enz, *Human Value Management* (San Francisco: Jossey-Bass, 1990), p. 10.

Epilogue

It is clear that best human asset management is a combination of beliefs, traits, and operating stratagems that separate the BHAM companies from others. However, behind the eight factors, there is a ferocious energy, intensely focused on goal achievement. Whether it be a process improvement, a financial objective, or a human factor, the BHAMs don't go halfway. In some companies, the culture may be very open and vocal, while in others, it is quiet and steady. Yet, in all cases, there is this underlying sense of strength, optimism, and determination that carries the organization along. Metaphorically, it is as though the enterprise were a ship riding a strong current that bears the vessel over the rapids of tough times and through the placid lakes of good times. It is difficult to communicate the feeling one gets inside these companies. To be sure, there are differences of opinion and even conflicts, but through it all, the current keeps flowing, bearing the enterprise toward its goals.

In any enterprise that is functioning smoothly, it is difficult to separate factors from time to time. In a symphony orchestra, periodically the woodwinds emerge with their sweet melodic tones only to recede again into the orchestral harmony. Then, the brass section or the timpani burst forth for a few bars before dropping back into the total sound. So it goes with an orchestra, and so it is with the BHAM factors. The base harmony is set by the dual value fixation, core strategy, and culture. Occasionally, communications programs and processes become visible before being superseded by partnering or the innovation drives needed to meet new demands. As I have described instances of the emergence of one or another of the factors, I have always kept in mind that each is simply one of eight instruments, playing a solo temporarily and then retreating into playing supportive harmony.

What's next? Will other factors emerge to join the eight? Or will apparently new drivers simply be the original eight in new dress? I can't foretell the future. And I'm not concerned about the life-cycle of the eight. The BHAM factors make more sense to me as organizational drivers than do reengineering, benchmarking, or quality programs. All of these are tools, useful when properly applied. But their focus is on process improvement—not on enterprise management. You can attend to process improvement and to organizational management and to enterprise building. It is not an either/or proposition. Each has its purpose and its potential values. I believe we have found something that is extremely fundamental, perhaps even seminal in the art and science of management. The lesson is: If it makes sense to you, use it and don't worry about tomorrow.

The Central Point

The most fundamental point I have tried to make here is that best practice is not something "out there." It should not matter to you in your company or to me in mine what any of the companies in this book have done at the *process* level. They are not perfect. What they did worked for them, more or less, most of the time. It helped them improve service, raise quality, or cut costs. It was and is the basis of their enterprise. But that was them, and then was then. Now, let's get down to what really matters: YOU and NOW.

> **BHAM Lesson:** *The guides to best practices for your organization are to be found* within *your organization.*

To some degree, your organization is unique. Your stakeholders: employees, customers, stockholders, communities, and competitors are different from those of any other organization. You know more about your stakeholders than anyone, so the knowledge of what will make you successful must reside within your organization. If it doesn't the only conclusion I can come to is that you are comatose—and I can't accept that. All you need to uncover what is best practice for you is a system for processing information about your stakeholders. That is what we have discovered and that is what I have tried to describe for you.

Take another look at Chapters 2 through 9. At the end of each chapter, I gave you a short checklist to start your creative juices flowing. Build your best practices by answering those questions. By definition, if you have valid answers to those questions, you will have the blueprint for being one of the best human asset management organizations.

Trying to take the path of least effort by emulating someone else's supposedly successful process or following the latest wizard and his magic wand is less useful than building on the central truths of good management. Consider the multitude of management schemes that have come along since 1950. How many times have you been skewered by the program of the month that turns out to be the flop of the year?

Wouldn't it make more sense to accept the fact that complex problems can't be solved by simplistic programs or popular panaceas? Instead, take the time you might put into chasing the newest miracle cure and put it into:

❑ Focusing your organization on value
❑ Making a long-term commitment to a core strategy
❑ Linking your culture to your systems
❑ Communicating everything that people should know
❑ Partnering
❑ Being mutually supportive
❑ Innovating and taking well-considered risks
❑ Never getting complacent

Be honest with yourself—and with me. If you did those eight things, wouldn't you have a terrific organization?

Good luck.

Let me know how it works for you. My e-mail address is: drja@sarains.com

Appendix

Best Human Asset Management Companies and Locations

The following companies are discussed in the text.
Ames Rubber Co., Hamburg, N.J.
Asten Group, Inc., Charleston, S.C.
AT&T Universal Card Services, Jacksonville, Fla.
Boy Scouts of America, Irving, Tex.
British Airways, London, England
Canadian Imperial Bank of Commerce, Toronto, Canada
Charleston Area Medical Center, Charleston, W.V.
Cigatam, Mexico City, Mexico
Consumer Value Stores, Woonsocket, R.I.
Electronic Data Systems, Dallas, Tex.
Financial Information Trust, Des Moines, Ia.
First Tennessee Bank, Memphis, Tenn.
Good Samaritan Health System, San Jose, Calif.
Griffins Foods Limited, Auckland, New Zealand
Gundersen Lutheran Hospital, LaCrosse, Wisc.
Hewlett-Packard, Palo Alto, Calif.
Holmes Regional Medical Center, Melbourne, Fla.
Iams Company, Dayton, Ohio
Lutheran General Hospital, Park Ridge, Ill.
Massachusetts Mutual Life, Springfield, Mass.
Mellon Bank, Pittsburgh, Penn.
Memorial Sloan-Kettering Cancer Center, New York, N.Y.

Micrografx, Dallas, Tex.
Pequiven, Caracas, Venezuela
Protective Life Corporation, Birmingham, Ala.
Provident Bank of Maryland, Baltimore, Md.
Prudential Property and Casualty Company, Newark, N.J.
Queensland Treasury, Brisbane, Australia
Raynet Corporation, Menlo Park, Calif.
Rosemont, Inc., Eden Prairie, Minn.
Sunbeam Plastics, Evansville, Ind.
TDS Computing Services, Madison, Wisc.
Texas Instruments, Dallas, Tex.
United Services Automobile Association, San Antonio, Tex.
Valley Children's Hospital, Fresno, Calif.

Index